Crisis Communications in Healthcare

Managing Difficult Times
Effectively

Society for Healthcare Strategy and Market Development®
of the American Hospital Association

ISBN: 0-9676441-6-X

Discounts on bulk quantities are available. For details or to place an order, call 1-800-242-2626 or order online at www.ahaonlinestore.com

Society for Healthcare Strategy and Market Development®
of the American Hospital Association

One North Franklin, Suite 2800
Chicago, IL 60606
312.422.3888

CONTENTS

LIST OF FIGURES

ACKNOWLEDGMENTS

Prior to September 11, 2001, we spoke of our preparedness for disaster—of our manuals and our disaster drills—and we claimed to be ready for anything. Today, we can only say that we are as prepared as we *can* be. We hope you will find this book helpful as you continue to take crisis preparedness to new levels.

This book truly was a team effort. It is based on a manuscript written by Marty Campanello, senior vice president, strategic planning and business development, BayHealth Medical Center, Dover, DE. Marty made extensive contributions to the manuscript. Special thanks go to Susan Alcorn, chief communications officer, Geisinger Health System, Danville, PA, and Fred Bagg, director, community relations and marketing, St. Francis Hospital & Health Centers, Indianapolis, IN, whose work is reflected throughout these pages. Credit also goes to Linda McGinity Jackson, vice president, public relations, Jewish Hospital Healthcare Services, Louisville. KY. Sally Benjamin Young, vice president, communications, Baxter International, Inc., Deerfield, IL, provided materials on developing strategic messages. In the communications technology section, we drew on the work of Scott Regan, vice president, marketing, strategic planning and human resources, Memorial Health, Savannah, GA. Patricia Usner, president, Usner & Associates, Philadelphia, PA, generously shared the post-September 11 hospital communications stories that she has compiled. And John Adams, director of institutional communications, Medical College of Ohio, Toledo, OH, provided material about media interviews based on MCO's *Media Training Guide,* as well as material about media access policies based on MCO's *Reporter's Notebook.*

We are indebted to all of our case study contributors. Each contributor has lived through healthcare crises from hurricanes to *E. coli* and has the scars and kudos to prove it. We are grateful that they shared their stories with us. Case study contributors include Marty Campanello; Judy Farrell, director, development and community relations, Palm Drive Hospital, Sebastopol, CA; Rose Glenn, vice president, Henry Ford Health System, Detroit, MI; Maureen Kersmarki, community relations director, Florida Hospital, Kissimmee, FL; Gary Kimsey, public relations coordinator, Poudre Valley Hospital, Fort Collins, CO; Michael Loyal, director, marketing and public relations, Indian River Memorial Hospital, Vero Beach, FL; Jeanine Nistler, director of communications, St. Cloud Hospital, St. Cloud, MN; Richard

Puff, associate director, Medical Center news office, Duke University Medical Center, Durham, NC; Kathy Rubado, director of marketing and public relations, Highlands Regional Medical Center, Prestonsburg, KY; Steve Rutledge, manager, external communications, Childrens Hospital Los Angeles, Los Angeles, CA; Steve Singer, senior vice president for communications, Dana-Farber Cancer Institute, Boston, MA; Anne Streeter, assistant vice president, Baptist Health South Florida, Coral Gables, FL; Adrienne Sylver, public relations consultant, Baptist Health South Florida, Coral Gables, FL; Charlotte Tharp, vice president, mission and outreach, Norton Healthcare, Louisville, KY; Clare Watson, vice president of marketing, CBR Public Relations, Orlando, FL; and Cliff Westerling, vice president, Canton-Potsdam Hospital, Potsdam, NY.

We would also like to thank our peer reviewers for their thoughtful and thorough review of the manuscript and their many strategically sound suggestions and comments: Becky Christian, senior vice president, strategic communications, WakeMed, Raleigh, NC; Mark Cohen, vice president, communications and public relations, VITAS Healthcare Corporation, Miami, FL; Don Giller, principal, D.R. Giller Associates, Lexington, MA; and Ken Trester, senior vice president, planning and marketing, Oakwood Healthcare System, Dearborn, MI.

Finally, thanks to Lauren Barnett, Society executive director, for her support throughout and strategic oversight of this project, and to Society staff member Karen Thomas, who conducted the case study interviews and served as managing editor.

Healthcare is an incredible field to "wrap your arms around," but it also provides a benefit to society that is unparalleled. With that in mind, let those of us who are members of the healthcare team strive to maintain a passion for what we do and compassion for those we serve.

INTRODUCTION

Although the healthcare delivered in America is the best in the world, healthcare organizations are not immune to adversity and crisis. Your work brings you into the most difficult times in the lives of patients and their families. Sickness, injury and death are *always* crises for those who are directly affected and—occasionally—such events lead to crises for the hospitals and health systems that care for them.

The word *crisis* has as many different definitions as there are kinds of emergencies and healthcare organizations. Some crises are the result of human errors or transgressions—a patient may die as the result of a medication error, a physician may be dismissed from the medical staff because of malpractice or incompetence. Disasters such as floods, hurricanes or airplane crashes present an entirely different kind of crisis.

Whatever the specifics of the incident may be, *crisis* in healthcare organizations always means the physical, emotional or privacy dimensions of someone's life have been adversely affected.

It is difficult—and often impossible—to predict when a crisis will occur. A few lucky souls will go through an entire career without ever experiencing one. On the other hand, a crisis might come before you have finished this paragraph or it might come tomorrow or next week.

No text can ever completely prepare you for "the big one." Nevertheless, the performance of a well-rehearsed and well-informed staff, which understands that its performance under extraordinary pressure may be even more important than its day-to-day performance, may spell the difference between successfully managing a crisis or unsuccessfully letting a crisis manage *you*—and your organization. Media attention relating to a crisis can be particularly damaging if not handled properly. In fact, the media can make a situation look a lot worse than it might actually be. Your organization's communications department must be prepared to deal with the media in virtually any difficult situation. Media can be a very positive ally; they often like to publicize your mission and stories about the people you serve. Therefore, good media relations are crucial.

The way a crisis is managed will largely determine the impact of the crisis on the organization. In other words, crisis communications can make a significant difference in restoring—perhaps even advancing—an organization's status in the community. One thing is certain: the more you know about crisis communications *before a crisis hits*, the better you and your organization will weather the storm.

This book will help your communications department take the lead in communicating with all key audiences during a crisis. By handling difficult situations well, healthcare organizations can continue to grow and flourish despite occasional obstacles and diversions.

PLANNING FOR A CRISIS

1.1. DEFINING *CRISIS*

A healthcare crisis is anything that suddenly or unexpectedly has adverse effects on a healthcare organization or its patients, staff or community.

Thus, if an elderly woman slips and falls outside the hospital entrance, there *may* be a crisis in the making. You did not expect it to happen, there may or may not have been anything you could have done to prevent it, but her misfortune will continue to affect the institution until any ensuing legal actions are resolved. Take it one step further—if the elderly woman happens to be the mother of the city's mayor—you definitely have the makings of a crisis on your hands—albeit a "small" one.

More than likely, however, when you say the word *crisis* to healthcare communicators, it is not the small things that come to mind first. The "big" things—such as airplane crashes, acts of terrorism and school shootings, to name just a few—are usually top-of-mind.

Because there is such a diverse array of crises that can affect healthcare organizations, it is helpful, for preparation purposes, to break them down into smaller categories. Crises, both big and small, may be categorized in a number of ways. Figure 1-1 provides a tool for assessing the severity of crisis situations based on their geographic scope, impact on operations, employee involvement, regulatory/accreditation/law enforcement agency involvement, the extent of public concern and the probable extent of media coverage.

Some incidents, such as storms that result in mass casualties and widespread property damage, are Level 3 crises by their very nature. Others start out as Level 1 emergencies that may escalate unnecessarily if they are not handled properly.

In addition to categorizing crises by their potential scope and impact, they may be classified by whether they originate inside or outside of the healthcare organization and by whether a medical emergency is involved. Saint Francis Hospital & Health Centers in Indianapolis, IN, uses such a classification, as shown in Figure 1-2. A taxonomy like this one is useful for differentiating types of crises based on the response that will be required. Saint Francis' Hospital Disaster Team will respond to all Class A crises. Class B and C crises may be dealt with by the Hospital Disaster Team or a specially created Crisis Team. This list also highlights the wide variety of crises for which hospitals and health systems must be prepared.

FIGURE 1-1
ASSESSING THE SEVERITY OF A CRISIS

	Level 1	Level 2	Level 3
GEOGRAPHIC SCOPE AND DURATION	Confined to a single facility or location.	Affects more than one location, but for a short period of time.	Affects the organization or the region for an indefinite period of time.
IMPACT ON OPERATIONS	Temporary. Confined primarily to one department. Operations will be normal in 12 to 24 hours.	Significant. Operations may shut down temporarily.	Extremely serious. Affected organization will be closed or will operate indefinitely at a fraction of normal levels.
EMPLOYEE INVOLVEMENT	Employees manage the response without major problems. They may be diverted from normal activities to handle the crisis.	Employees need support from senior management and/or external resources.	Employees need support from senior management and/or external resources. Total workforce involved. May need support of health-care professionals from other organizations.
REGULATORY/ ACCREDITATION/ LAW ENFORCEMENT AGENCY INVOLVEMENT	Minimal concern. Phone call and/or written report may be required.	Appropriate agencies will actively investigate the situation and issue fines/citations. Applicable sanctions are minimal to moderate.	Appropriate agencies will actively investigate the situation and issue fines/citations. Applicable sanctions are serious, e.g., loss of Medicare/Medicaid certification; unit, service line or facility closure.
PUBLIC CONCERN	Limited to parties who are directly involved in the situation.	Some public anxiety. Relatives of patients, community residents and others may contact the hospital for information on an urgent basis.	Substantial public anxiety. Volume of calls received strains or exceeds the organization's normal capacity.
LIKELY MEDIA COVERAGE	Maximum publicity is one day of local news coverage.	Regional or statewide wire service and trade press.	National or international media interest. Major newspapers, TV, radio and magazines cover the incident.

FIGURE 1-2
SAMPLE HOSPITAL AND HEALTH SYSTEM CRISIS CATEGORIES

CLASS A

▦ **Natural Disasters**
  - blizzards
  - earthquakes
  - floods
  - tornadoes

▦ **External Disasters/Medical Emergencies**
  - chemical exposure
  - epidemic of disease
  - explosions
  - fires
  - large-scale poisoning
  - multiple-victim accidents
      (car, bus, train, plane crashes)
  - nuclear fallout
  - riots
  - structural collapse
  - toxic radiation

CLASS B

▦ **Internal Disasters/Medical Emergencies**
  - death of key personnel
  - death of religious personnel
  - disease epidemics
  - explosions
  - fire
  - large-scale food poisoning
  - large-scale infections
  - multiple administrative deaths
  - terrorist activity

CLASS C

▦ **Internal Disasters/ Nonmedical Emergencies**
  - bomb threats
  - accusations from consumer group
  - death of a patient or employee under criminal or mysterious circumstances
  - State Board of Health declared emergency
  - strikes
  - union activity
  - citations by regulatory agencies
  - criminal activity within the hospital (rape, robbery, shooting, kidnapping, hostage taking)
  - malpractice suit or accusation against hospital or physician on staff
  - well-known public figure as patient
  - problem with major supplier (construction, drug, equipment)
  - power failure
  - major mechanical failure
  - unique or unusual medical stories (multiple births or medical rarities)
  - embezzlement
  - misuse of funds
  - Internet or computer virus, hack into medical records, etc.

Source: St. Francis Hospital & Health Centers, Indianapolis, IN
www.stfrancishospitals.org.

It is useful to differentiate between crises that require the hospital to provide emergency medical care and those that do not. The latter category includes the crises that are listed in Figure 1-2 under "Class C, Internal Disasters/Nonmedical Emergencies." For the most part, such crises will not require the involvement of large numbers of your organization's staff. In fact, beyond the administration and senior management, communications and legal staff, a relatively small number of people will be involved. But that is *not* to say that such internal/nonmedical crises can be treated lightly or ignored—quite the contrary. While massive trauma tests an institution's infrastructure and its physical stamina, dealing with an internal crisis tests its mettle, ethics and sometimes its integrity.

Internal/nonmedical crises differ from other types of crises in the scope of communication that will be involved.

- A major trauma or natural disaster may result in large numbers of media descending on your institution at one time; the internal/nonmedical crisis probably will, at least over time, involve fewer media at any given point.

- A multiple-casualty disaster requires that emphasis be placed on communicating with the media and the public about the condition of victims. An internal/nonmedical crisis mandates that you turn your primary communications efforts internally first to employees, medical staff, hospital board members and volunteers—then follow up with communications to the media and the general public.

- The involvement of your organization's legal counsel is limited when a natural disaster strikes; in the internal/nonmedical crisis, the involvement of legal counsel and risk management staff is often critically important.

- Much of the communication during a medical crisis takes place via news briefings and conferences. In contrast, much of the media communications during an internal/nonmedical crisis occurs in one-on-one settings with reporters. Whereas reporters are themselves a high-profile collective audience during a medical crisis, positive outcomes to other crises often are the result of one-on-one meetings with editors, editorial boards, publishers and other key opinion leaders in the community, including elected officials.

- Multiple-casualty disasters have a discrete beginning and ending, at least from the hospital's perspective. Other crises may appear to go away, only to resurface each time there is a new revelation—such as a court appearance or the filing of a critical report.

Internal/nonmedical crises include adverse events that must be reported to regulatory and/or accreditation agencies. Since 1996, the Joint Commission on Accreditation of Healthcare Organizations (JCAHO) has had a policy that requires reporting of unexpected occurrences known as "sentinel events." City, county and state health departments and other regulatory organizations may also mandate reporting adverse events.

SENTINEL EVENTS

The Joint Commission defines *sentinel events* as unexpected occurrences that involve death, serious physical or psychological injury, or the risk thereof. In JCAHO parlance, a sentinel event can result from errors of commission or errors of omission. Errors of *commission* are those wherein the wrong action is taken, for example, giving a patient the wrong medication; errors of *omission* are those in which a required action is delayed or not taken, for instance, *not* giving a medication.

Examples of Sentinel Events That Are Voluntarily Reportable under the Joint Commission's Sentinel Event Policy

- Any patient death, paralysis, coma or other major permanent loss of function associated with a medication error.
- Any suicide of a patient in a setting where the patient is housed around-the-clock, including suicides following elopement from such a setting.
- Any elopement, i.e., unauthorized departure, of a patient from an around-the-clock care setting resulting in a temporally related death (suicide or homicide) or major permanent loss of function.
- Any procedure on the wrong patient, wrong side of the body or wrong organ.
- Any intrapartum (related to the birth process) maternal death.
- Any perinatal death unrelated to a congenital condition in an infant having a birth weight greater than 2,500 grams.
- Assault, homicide or other crime resulting in patient death or major permanent loss of function.
- A patient fall that results in death or major permanent loss of function as a direct result of the injuries sustained in the fall.
- Hemolytic transfusion reaction involving major blood group incompatibilities.

Note: *An adverse outcome that is directly related to the natural course of the patient's illness or underlying condition, e.g., terminal illness present at the time of presentation, is not reportable except for suicide in, or following elopement from, a 24-hour care setting (see preceding list).*

Examples of Events That Are Not Reportable to the Joint Commission

- Any "near miss."
- Full return of limb or bodily function to the same level as prior to the adverse event by discharge or within two weeks of the initial loss of said function.
- Any sentinel event that has not affected a recipient of care (patient, client, resident).
- Medication errors that do not result in death or major permanent loss of function.
- Suicide other than in an around-the-clock care setting or following elopement from such a setting.
- A death or loss of function following a discharge "against medical advice (AMA)."
- Unsuccessful suicide attempts.
- Unintentionally retained foreign body without major permanent loss of function.
- Minor degrees of hemolysis with no clinical sequelae.

As of January 2002, 69.2 percent of all sentinel events reported to the JCAHO were *self-reported*, but 12.8 percent come to the JCAHO's attention through media reports. Other sources are complaints (8.8 percent), accreditation surveys (6.1 percent) and other sources, including government agencies (3.0 percent).

Source: *Sentinel Event Alert*, Issue 4, May 11, 1998 and *Sentinel Event Statistics*, January 23, 2002. Joint Commission on Accreditation of Healthcare Organizations, www.jcaho.org.

While it is true that any of these disparate crises can—and do—happen, the risks associated with particular kinds of crises vary in different kinds of healthcare organizations and different regions of the country. Statistics tell us that some crises, such as airplane crashes, are low risk altogether. Most hospitals and health systems have risk management departments that can provide valuable information about organization-specific risks. Hospitals and health systems should invest most of their crisis communications planning efforts into preparing for the crises that are most likely to occur and/or have the greatest potential for doing damage to the organization's image and its relationships with key constituents.

Figure 1-3 provides a tool for assessing the likelihood of various crises and the potential damage they may cause. The crises that merit the most preparation are those that would be assigned to the upper righthand quadrant—high potential damage and high likelihood of occurrence. The crises that require the least amount of preparation are those you would assign to the lower lefthand quadrant—low potential damage and low chance of occurrence.

FIGURE 1-3
CRISIS SCENARIO RISK MATRIX

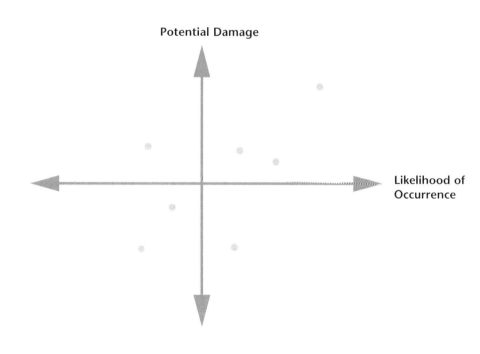

1.2. WHY YOU NEED A CRISIS COMMUNICATIONS PLAN

A glance at the list of crises in Figure 1-2 may be enough to convince you of the need for a plan. Chances are, you would not want to tackle any of those problems without one. Here are a few more reasons for having—and practicing—a crisis communications plan.

- *A crisis communications plan is a regulatory and accreditation requirement.* The Joint Commission requires hospitals to establish, update and implement crisis communications plans. The Joint Commission has focused on emergency management planning in the wake of September 11 and the subsequent anthrax incidents. The December 2001 issue of *Joint Commission Perspectives* was dedicated to emergency management planning (Joint Commission 2001). JCAHO issued new emergency management standards in January 2001, which include recommendations about staff training in media relations and crowd control.

- *A crisis communications plan is a high-profile example of your hospital or health system's commitment to quality.* Healthcare organizations in the first decade of the 21st century will increasingly be competing on the basis of quality. Employers and other purchasers of care will demand it. A comprehensive crisis communications plan symbolizes a hospital's high-quality emergency care. Crisis communications plans need not be proprietary—after all, these plans exist for the benefit of the community. Many hospitals post sections of their crisis communications plans on their websites. This serves as a visible reminder that they are ready to deal with any crisis that may arise.

- *A crisis communications plan helps ensure that staff are aware of and understand their roles in times of crisis.* The best way of standardizing staff orientation and education about crisis management is to have all relevant crisis-related information compiled in one place and to base training on that document. Crises are inherently chaotic; a written plan can help staff feel centered and in control of the situation. It can also help avert territorial disputes among staff at a time when such squabbles have the greatest potential for doing damage.

- *A crisis communications plan can enhance media relations.* When you give the media access to your crisis communications policies, they have a better idea of what to expect and of what they can reasonably request. This prevents misunderstandings that can become secondary crises in themselves.

The outcome of crisis management is a function of the amount of time, effort and education the organization has put into thinking, planning and educating staff about what to do in an emergency. Many crises can be successfully handled by good management based on sound principles and reinforced by lots of repetitive drill.

Case Study 1.1, *Tornadoes in Hurricane Country*, at the end of this chapter, shows how vital it is to practice your crisis communications plan. As the public relations director in this case observes, "Everything we'd ever rehearsed for in a disaster drill happened." As luck would have it, the last disaster drill had been staged two weeks before the tornadoes hit.

Case Study 1.2, *The Perfect (Ice) Storm*, shows how important it is for your plan to be flexible. Throughout the weeks following the storm, employees worked jobs they had never worked before—for example, the director of human resources and the president worked in the kitchen and on the nursing units. Communications professionals, like everyone else on the hospital team, will often be called on to do whatever needs to be done in a crisis—and somehow find ways to get their own work done, too.

1.3. COMPONENTS OF A CRISIS COMMUNICATIONS PLAN

Most healthcare crisis communications plans should include the elements listed below. The order of these components within the plan will vary from one organization to another. And this list is just a starting point—you may wish to combine certain plan elements or add others based on your organization's specific needs. (*The number in parentheses following each topic indicates the section in this book where additional information may be found.*)

- *Procedures and contact information for notifying public relations staff in the event of a crisis.* ("Communications" staff and "public relations" staff are used interchangeably throughout this book.) This section of the plan provides complete contact information for all public relations staff members and a procedure for notifying them of an impending crisis. (2.2)

- *Roles and responsibilities of specific public relations staffers, by organizational title and name of incumbent.* This ensures that everyone knows who is responsible for what, ahead of time, and provides step-by-step information for navigating the crisis. This section should specify the chain of command in the event that the CEO is unavailable. (2.1)

- *Contact information for various crisis communications audiences.* Prospective audiences include the media, the public, employees, physicians, board members, community groups, public health authorities, law enforcement and public officials and a host of others. Union leaders and representatives represent another prospective audience, although communications with these groups are often handled by human resources or labor relations staff. Contact information should be maintained for various resource people within the organization who help public relations staff with information technology, telecommunications services, security, food and beverage, photocopier repair and other support services as well as key medical and other clinical personnel. This section of the plan provides contact information for these individuals and groups. (2.2)

- *Special communications vehicles and technologies that may be activated in a crisis.* These may include toll-free hotlines for the media and/or the public, the hospital's internal web page, or intranet, and the hospital website, among others. (2.2)

- *Communications-related roles and responsibilities of noncommunications staff.* This section provides information about what employees outside the public relations department should do if they receive media calls. (3.2)

- *Media policies and procedures.* These may include policies about media access to patients, patient interview prerequisites, access by photographers and television crews and disaster-related information. (3.2)

- *Message log.* The message log is a written record of all media contacts, including follow-up calls, as recorded on media inquiry forms. This section of the plan describes procedures for fielding media calls and recording media contacts. (3.3)

- *Policies and procedures for releasing information about the condition of patients.* The Society publishes specific guidelines on this topic, which are reprinted in Appendix B. (2.3)

- *Location of and specifications for the media center.* The media may spend hours, days or even longer in a central room that you designate and furnish for their use during a crisis. Another room, such as a physician's lounge or classroom, often doubles as a media center. Specific guidelines for setting up the media center can expedite this process during a crisis when time is at a premium. (3.7)

You may also want to include "refresher" material such as "Do's and Don'ts of Emergency Public Relations" in an appendix to the plan. (Appendix A)

1.4. CHARACTERISTICS OF GOOD CRISIS COMMUNICATIONS PLANS

Good crisis communications plans are as different as the organizations that develop them—but they have certain basic characteristics in common. Good plans are:

- **Easy to understand.** An easy-to-understand plan translates directly into an easy-to-*follow* plan. And in many crises—especially the "big" ones—many people have roles to play; they need to know these roles and why they are important.

- **Simple and specific.** Plans that work provide individuals and departments with clear, simple, understandable roles.

- **Easy to implement.** If you ever receive a call from the state police saying there has been a pile-up on the highway and you will have a dozen people in your emergency room in the next few minutes, you will truly appreciate this aspect of a good plan. Time—or the lack of it—will almost always be as big a problem as the crisis itself. Develop your plan so it can be put into effect immediately.

- **Clear in the delineation of responsibilities and accountabilities.** There is only one way to avoid territorial disputes in the middle of a crisis: spell out who does what, when, how and with whom *before* the crisis hits.

- **Flexible.** The plan should be flexible enough to work at any and all times—even when you cannot. Designate backup persons to handle media relations and other key crisis communication responsibilities in the event that the primary staff are unavailable. Depending on the size of your organization and your department, backup staffers may have little or no public relations experience. Find the time to brief these people on crisis communications—in general and in organization-specific terms. They should be as familiar with the plan as you are. When your plan changes, make sure your designated backups understand the changes.

- **Integrated into facilitywide crisis/disaster plans.** The crisis communications plan is not synonymous with the organizational disaster plan. The latter deals with a myriad of logistical issues, ranging from checking the facility's generators on a monthly basis and ensuring that the battery-powered stairwell-lighting system is fully functional to maintaining a stock of emergency provisions. Crisis communications plans typically are integrated into the organization's overall crisis/disaster planning process, rather than vice versa. The communications plan is a vitally important part of an overall crisis/disaster management strategy.

1.5. Practicing the Plan: The Key to Success

When it comes to crisis communications plans, "use it or lose it" should be the guiding principle.

The more you practice the skills, techniques and systems that make up a crisis communications plan, the greater the likelihood of a smooth implementation should the plan ever need to be called into action.

But how do you practice the unknown? You would organize your response to a tornado one way—quite differently from how you would respond to allegations of malpractice. You would deal with an impaired employee quite differently from the way you would handle a malpractice suit. And even if you knew what to practice, how do you do it with minimal disruption to the mission of the organization and its patients? There are three basic approaches to disaster drills:

- **Announced, scheduled and scripted.** Some organizations choose to stage a disaster drill complete with a script, to be held at a designated date and time. The drawback of this approach is that it eliminates any possibility of testing response to sudden events. In addition, a script—as opposed to guidelines—denies participants the flexibility they will need to respond to a real-life crisis.

- **Localized, planned, promoted and flexible.** A good example of this type of "dry run" is the process that communities use when the relevant agencies band together to plan and execute a mock disaster drill involving multiple organizations—law enforcement, media, hospitals, first responders and others. Because all parties know that the drill will take place, your crisis communications team can gain some experience implementing their roles. Usually, the details of such drills are restricted to date and time; the exact nature of the mock disaster is not revealed. This adds credence to the drill.

- **Targeted and contained.** For example, the designated senior communications officer could initiate the crisis notification process (*see Section* 2.2) to test its effectiveness. No other departments are involved; there is no need to escalate the test beyond one specific function.

No matter which approach your organization takes, someone from the communications team should periodically check to ensure that crisis communications supplies are intact and that telephone and Internet connections in the designated media center are operational.

1.6. AFTERMATH: REFLECT, REVISIT, REVISE

After the crisis has passed—or after the drill is over—every plan should be given a thorough post-mortem analysis. What worked? What did *not* work? Who did something that clearly should have been done by others?

Solicit feedback and suggestions from everyone who was involved with communications during the drill or the incident. Assembling the crisis communication team and reviewing what worked, what did not work and what could have been done better is an important step in developing an up-to-date, effective communications plan for the next time.

In your debriefing process after a crisis is over, be sure to ask the media about their satisfaction with their accommodations as well as access to phone lines, fax machines and the Internet. Media can also provide valuable feedback about how effectively information was (or was not) delivered during the crisis. This is a good time to review the lists of reporters and other media representatives who covered the story and add any new names to your media database. If you have served them well during a time of crisis, they may be more receptive to your suggestions for stories under better circumstances.

After the review is over, the public relations team should take responsibility for determining what changes, if any, should be made to the communications plan. A team member should be assigned to update, reprint and distribute hardcopies of the revised plan. Do not rely on electronic retrieval or distribution, which require that recipients take the extra step of printing out the replacement pages. Briefly summarize the changes in a cover memo in the simplest possible language. Let employees, other audiences and the appropriate authorities know that you have enhanced the plan and urge them to review the changes.

What kinds of changes are typically made after the crisis plan has been implemented? We interviewed more than a dozen public relations and communications professionals who have helped guide their hospitals and health systems through all kinds of crises. Their stories are told in the case studies that appear at the end of each chapter. Following are a few of the practical and logistical factors our case study respondents would like to change if they could do it over again. Learn from their experiences and incorporate these items into your crisis communications plan sooner rather than later.

- **Be prepared to live through a crisis without electricity**. Having a backup generator does not necessarily mean there will be enough power for your computers. Make sure your disaster plan would work if you were without computers for an extended period. Maintain hard copies of important documents, including calling lists and other emergency planning documents. If you have moved beyond paper forms for certain administrative functions, do not throw them all away. Keep a supply for use in an emergency—and periodically remind staff how to use them. The staff at Canton Potsdam Hospital in Potsdam, NY, offer this tip after surviving an ice storm that knocked out power for weeks.

—See Case Study 1.2, *The Perfect (Ice) Storm.*

- **Let the pictures tell the story**. In a crisis that involves helping your community through a natural disaster such as a flood or a hurricane, assign a staff member to take pictures of the hospital team in action. Such crises often become pivotal events in community history. After Hurricane Andrew struck South Florida in 1992, the public relations staff at Baptist Health South Florida wished they had taken more pictures for their employee newsletter and other publications. This is a role for the team historian. (*See Figure 2-1.*) Baptist's advice: "Take more pictures than you think you will need."

    —See Case Study 4.3,*"Andrew Zero, Baptist Won."*

- **Establish a "reserve" staff so you can call in the troops when they are needed**. In a high-profile case, the more help you have, the better. Childrens Hospital Los Angeles (CHLA) discovered this in the aftermath of an internationally publicized shooting at the local Jewish Community Center that left four people injured, including three children. CHLA pulled in a dozen people to escort media to the right place, ensure that media stayed out of the intensive care area, log phone calls and keep the entire process under control. Who would you call for help if all of your staff were already mobilized? Make the arrangements now and put them in the plan.

    —See Case Study 2.3, *A Hate Crime Against Children.*

- **Identify an alternate—larger—place for the media to gather if your designated media room is too small**. When the media showed up in droves after a school bus accident in 1999, Indian River Memorial Hospital in Vero Beach, FL, learned the hard way that its designated media room was too small. Now the hospital's boardroom is used as a media room. From time to time, review the appropriateness of rooms you have designated for special groups in times of crisis. How many people can the room hold comfortably? How does that number compare with the number who might *actually come on site* in a high-profile crisis? Choose a larger backup site to serve as your media room in case it is needed.

    —See Case Study 3.2, *School Bus Accident.*

Read the "lessons learned" sections of the case studies throughout this book for more experience-based advice about what to include in your crisis communications plan.

CASE STUDY 1.1
TORNADOES IN HURRICANE COUNTRY

The seven tornadoes that hit central Florida at midnight on February 23, 1998, were among the worst in history—Level 4 tornadoes with winds in excess of 200 miles per hour.

Of the 42 people killed, 25 were from rural Osceola County—where Florida Hospital Kissimmee is located—and 24 of the 25 lived in mobile homes. Adding insult to injury, the storm also caused $37 million in other property damage.

In all, 40 storm victims were treated at the hospital—25 of them arriving in just two-and-a-half hours. Twelve were admitted; 11 were eventually discharged and one died a week after the storm. (All of this activity was in addition to the hospital's normal patient volume. For a 100-bed hospital with a 12-bed emergency department during the busy winter season, the numbers alone were staggering. But the numbers tell only part of the story.)

Employees will never forget the scene: ambulance after ambulance pulling up to the emergency department doors; EMS staff unloading seriously injured patients and then rushing out to find more victims, and dozens of stunned and mud-covered patients and family members filling the treatment area and lobbies.

The hospital operator called public relations director Maureen Kersmarki at 1 a.m. with a mass casualty alert. Fifteen minutes later, the hospital instituted its major disaster plan. (Just two weeks earlier, the hospital had tested its readiness with a disaster drill. "Everything and more we'd ever rehearsed for in a disaster drill happened," recalls Maureen "We were all prepared for the disaster, but not its intensity, duration or emotional impact.")

Maureen hurried through an eerie post-storm quiet to get to the hospital, driving along flooded roads and watching for downed trees and power lines. She arrived at 2:10 a.m., exactly two minutes before the floodgates opened and the first patients arrived. To keep track of patients, the admitting office logged them in a patient log that had been developed by public relations staff – and used a runner to get updates to the command center, public relations and social services staff every 15 minutes.

By 3 a.m., the calls started pouring in from worried relatives. The phone lines were jammed, so social workers began exchanging Florida Hospital's patient lists with other area hospitals so family members could be directed to the right hospital or told that the people they were looking for were not at any hospital.

By 4:30 a.m., the media calls started. By 8 a.m., there had been 30 media calls, including live telephone interviews with local television and radio, and even the BBC. In the next 24 hours, there were a total of 100 calls (more than 50 more came later in the week) from local, regional, national and even international media outlets. In all, during the week after the disaster, the public relations staff facilitated 15 patient interviews with the media.

Just before noon on the second day, public relations relief staff arrived to help Maureen and another employee who had worked all night. (One benefit of being part of a 1452-bed, six-hospital system is the ability to get help from the system's marketing and public relations department when needed.)

As often happens after a disaster, many people, including emergency responders and concerned residents, wanted to help and to visit those who had been injured in the storm. The hospital facilitated emotional visits by city and county EMS staff to patients they had rescued, after first securing the patient's permission. But school groups and other Good Samaritans who wanted to visit were graciously declined to protect patient privacy and provide patients needed rest and recovery time. Essays written by local high school students were given to the nursing supervisor for distribution to patients–not hand-delivered.

Unfortunately, there were incidents of reporters slipping into the hospital under the guise of being visitors. And days after the storm, a small, out-of-town newspaper created its own "scoop" by setting up a "reunion" between a rescuer and an unsuspecting hospital patient—along with the cameras.

While the hospital's primary mission was to care for the injured, it also had to take care of its own. Eleven employees lost homes. Other employees chipped in to raise $6,400, which was deposited in a "Care to Share" fund for employees affected by the storm. The hospital's employee assistance program provided individualized help and support to those who had been affected by the storm.

Employees and the hospital also helped the community recovery effort in many ways, ranging from volunteering at Red Cross centers and providing nursing support at community shelters to working at the Osceola County Disaster Command Center and helping with the cleanup efforts. Pharmacy employees filled prescriptions for Council on Aging clients who lost their medication in the storm. The hospital donated 50 first aid kits to the area disaster command center and food for 2,000 people who attended a citywide memorial service or were helping with the clean up.

LESSONS LEARNED

- The patient log is the key to being able to quickly answer questions about the whereabouts and conditions of patients. A Microsoft Word or Excel spreadsheet works best. Each patient should be assigned a number in the order of arrival so total patient counts can be kept current. At some point, the list may need to be sorted alphabetically.

- Communicators should always actively participate in hospital disaster planning. Day-to-day responsibilities and deadlines often make disaster planning seem like a low priority—but when a disaster actually happens the drills prove their worth.

- Set clear goals for the public relations disaster plan. Because Florida Hospital's case management staff handles communication with patients' family members, the public relations department's goals were limited to external communication and included the following: manage the media, obtain positive press coverage, build positive media relations, position the hospital as a community partner and help the employee family.

- Keep your public relations disaster plan current and flexible. Hospitals in different areas of the country tend to prepare for the disasters that are most likely to occur in their region. The Florida Hospital plan was traditionally focused on hurricane preparedness. In this case, the hospital had to respond to tornadoes—similar to hurricanes in many ways, but without the advance warning.

- Drill enough so staff response will become automatic when the inevitable middle-of-the-night mass casualty call comes.

- Make sure there is some flexibility about where to locate the command center. Some disasters could affect the hospital itself, or your designated locations could be commandeered for other purposes.

- Encourage administration to bring in Critical Incident Stress Debriefing teams after the disaster, and attend them yourself. All of you are carrying a huge emotional burden—far more than you realize.

- Stay focused on public relations' role and goals.

- Make the disaster plan adaptable—and available—for relief public relations staff.

- Make and stock a few "disaster boxes" that include a radio with a TV band, a cassette or microcassette recorder, flashlights, telephone lists, spare batteries, office supplies and other essentials along with copies of the disaster plan and forms such as media logs, patient logs and photo releases.

- Keep a list of important locations such as the rooms that will serve as the media and family areas.

- Bring your cell phone and cell phone charger, even though they can't be used inside the hospital in most cases–major disasters often mean you won't be able to call in or out on hospital phone lines.

- If other public relations staff relieves you—especially if they come from outside your institution—make sure you personally introduce them to the nursing supervisor, the patient registration personnel and other key individuals. These folks are happy to help—if they know who they are helping.

- Call in the public relations relief troops early—even when you don't think you need to. Working in a crisis is physically and emotionally exhausting. You're running on adrenaline. If you try to hang in there too long, you will crash and it will be very difficult to come back for your next shift. Plus, in cases like this, it's not over for days—the media frenzy continues until the very last patient is discharged days or even weeks later.

CASE STUDY 1.1

CASE STUDY 1.2
THE PERFECT (ICE) STORM

January 1998: An unusually severe ice storm struck a small area of northern New York, resulting in four days of continuous rain that immediately turned to four *inches* of ice. Telephone poles snapped. Electrical poles collapsed. Many roads were impassable due to fallen trees that had collapsed under the weight of the ice.

During the storm, Canton-Potsdam Hospital was a safe haven in many ways. Fortunately, the hospital had recently purchased a backup generator that provided heat and most necessary lighting for the 94-bed hospital. Everything, that is, except power for the computers.

As the rest of the region came to a virtual standstill, Canton-Potsdam took care of more patients than ever before. For two weeks after the ice storm, the emergency room volume doubled from the normal level of 40 to 50 patients per day. Every floor was at or over capacity, with some beds in the hallways. To concentrate all available resources on storm-related injuries and illnesses, elective surgery and nonemergency scheduled outpatient services were postponed.

Marshalling the resources needed to run the hospital was, in itself, an extremely difficult and sometimes impossible process because of the difficulty employees had traveling between home and work. Administrative staff set up transport teams of four-wheel-drive vehicle owners who were willing to try to bring hospital employees to work and take discharged patients home.

Many employees camped out in the hospital, sleeping on makeshift cots in classrooms and conference rooms, sharing cramped quarters with rescue squads and National Guard troops that had been dispatched to help.

Throughout the crisis, employees worked jobs they had never worked before—the director of human resources and the president worked in the kitchen and on the nursing units. At one point, there was an excess of volunteers because staff wanted to bring their family members into the safe harbor of the hospital and have them help out.

Four area colleges also served as shelters, but many area residents, particularly seniors, wanted to stay at the hospital, because it was both familiar and reassuring. Not everyone could stay, obviously, so hospital employees had to market the college shelters to area residents.

Communications were important during this crisis. A physician provided cold-weather tips on local radio stations, which were also the primary medium the hospital used to contact its employees. Information was repeated frequently, with news bulletins issued every hour.

Internal printed news reports provided accurate information and helped boost morale. These reports summarized the status of several important concerns: power, water, travel, supplies, mail and special services such as emergency check cashing, "credit" in the hospital cafeteria, and temporary payroll policies for employees who worked overtime or were unable to get in to work. Administration authorized some employees to go into the community to help out, and counted the work as though they were at the hospital. This helped direct needed resources to smaller shelters.

LESSONS LEARNED

- Having a backup generator does not necessarily mean there will be enough power for computers. Make sure your disaster plan will work if you are without computers for an extended period.

- Maintain hard copies of important documents, including calling lists and other emergency planning documents.

- If you have moved beyond paper forms for certain administrative functions, do not throw them all away. Keep a supply for use in an emergency and periodically remind staff how to use them.

- If you do use paper records for tasks that are customarily computerized, file one copy and keep another one for data entry once the systems are back up.

- If your medical records department is in a windowless area, keep a stock of flashlights on hand to facilitate finding files on darkened shelves.

- Hold disaster planning team meetings every day. Canton-Potsdam attributes much of the successful handling of the ice storm crisis to these daily meetings. Summarize the meetings and post the summaries where all employees can read them. E-mail the summaries when possible.

- In formulating a disaster plan, think beyond your own four walls to the entire community. Keep an updated contact list of your counterparts at other area hospitals as well as community and governmental agencies. Daily meetings of leaders in the community (hospitals, colleges, police, fire, rescue, Red Cross and representatives from utility companies) brought resources where they were most needed, and created a channel for accurate information in uncertain times.

- Before an emergency happens, the human resources department should establish or review policies for paying employees who are unable to come to work due to weather/power problems or employees who are told *not to* come in to work because of such concerns. During the emergency, communicate these policies to employees actively and often.

- You *can* have too much of a good thing—even volunteers. Start thinking early on about ways excess volunteer energy could be channeled elsewhere.

- In a crisis that involves power or water outages, employees may be seeking shelter for their families and, in some cases, even their pets. If the hospital is unable to provide such shelter, be prepared with good alternatives, including kennel care. These items will be part of your internal communications campaign.

CRISIS COMMUNICATIONS: THE BASICS

- Who should be on your crisis communications team?
- In a crisis, what individuals or groups will you want to reach?
- What communications media or technologies should be used to reach them?
- *And last but not least—what should you say?*

These are the basics of crisis communications and the focus of this section.

2.1. ASSEMBLING THE TEAM

A team of knowledgeable professionals encompassing several disciplines will be required for effective communications to take place during a crisis. Figure 2-1 provides a list of suggested crisis communications team members and their respective roles. These roles should be assigned well in advance. Some team members—such as legal counsel and outside communications counsel—will only be called in when needed. Others who are not on this list—infectious disease specialists or physicians with other specific expertise, for example—may be recruited on an as-needed basis.

This team should be advised that it might be convened at any time of day or night in the event of a crisis. Even though their role as a team may never come about, they must be prepared to function as a crisis communications team on a moment's notice.

Also, keep in mind that crisis communications must reflect the policies and strategies your organization will follow—and those policies and strategies often come from the CEO and executive management. The chief communications officer must know the chain of command in a crisis—who is responsible for strategy in the event that the CEO is not available.

Figure 2-1
Crisis Communications Team Members, Roles and Responsibilities

Function on Crisis Communications Team	Organizational Position	Responsibilities
Crisis communications coordinator	Chief communications executive	Coordinates activities of all others on the communications team.
Internal communications coordinator	Employee communications staff	Keeps staff (including employees, medical staff, volunteers, suppliers and other internal audiences) informed.
External/media communications coordinator	Chief communications executive or media relations specialist	Takes responsibility for ensuring that media needs are met.
Patient/family communications	Other communications or marketingstaff members, nurse executives,chaplains or pastoral care staff,patient advocates or patientrepresentatives	Keeps friends and family of disaster victims informed. Serves as a liaison between families and the organization.
Medical adviser	Medical director, chief of clinical service, other physician leaders	Explains/interprets medical issues for other team members; serves as or selects a spokesperson to address medical issues with the media
Legal counsel	In-house or outside legal counsel	Advises and assists with legal and regulatory issues.
Outside communications counsel.	Public relations/marketing agency	Works at the specific direction of staff In some cases, however, outside communications counsel will serve *as* staff.
Support staff	Gathered from the communications departments and elsewhere throughout the organization	Provide administrative support when and where needed.
Web staff (outside contract staff as needed)	Inter- and intranet staff with assistance from information technology department	Ensure that all relevant and appropriate information is posted immediately to the organization's electronic distribution media.
Historian	Communications or marketing staff member or other volunteer	Keeps a written record of events. Shoots photographs and videos to create a pictorial record, when appropriate.

2.2. IDENTIFYING AUDIENCES AND CHOOSING COMMUNICATIONS VEHICLES

All of the organization's professional communicators—media relations, employee communications, public relations and marketing communications—should work together as a team during a crisis to convey a unified and coherent message. There are many audiences to consider during a crisis, each with its own needs and interests. When we think about crisis communications, we tend to focus on the media. But the reality is that internal audiences such as employees, physicians and board members can be equally important. And there are many key external audiences besides the media, such as large employers and employer coalitions, community service agencies and managed care organizations. Crisis communications audiences are listed in Figure 2-2. To reach all of these groups efficiently and effectively, the organization will need to draw on the specialized expertise each of its communications professionals has to offer.

Notifying the Crisis Team

The first group you need to reach in a crisis is the crisis team itself. It is imperative for the crisis team to convene promptly to assess the situation and prepare for inquiries from the media and other audiences. It is very important to maintain updated contact information for all crisis team members, as well as outside audiences. Current contact information for each team member, including alternates, should be distributed to all crisis team members and one copy should be kept with the crisis communications plan. Updating these contact lists is a tedious task that too often falls to the bottom of the priority list. Link this chore to a recurring date or event in the administrative cycle and schedule it on your calendar to make sure it gets done.

Many organizations establish a "calling tree" or pyramid where one individual (often the nursing supervisor or administrator-on-call) is designated to invoke the disaster plan. The initiator calls one or two other people who, in turn, each call others, and so forth. A similar calling tree should be developed for the crisis communications team. Following are some tips for using the calling tree effectively.

* Know and use team members' home phone, cell phone and pager numbers.
* Because this team is relatively small, be sure that the "tree" makes provisions for employees who cannot be reached because of vacation or travel schedules.
* Designate someone on your staff to maintain the calling tree. Ask team members to notify that person when their contact information changes. However, this should not replace regularly scheduled contact list updates.
* Test the system regularly. Inform team members that you will—at various times—test the system for effectiveness.

A small, but growing number of hospitals and health systems have equipped all of their managers with handheld devices such as Palm Pilots that are meant to replace calling trees as the primary communications vehicle during a crisis.

FIGURE 2-2
CRISIS COMMUNICATIONS AUDIENCES AND COMMUNICATIONS VEHICLES

Audience	Potential Communications Vehicles	Notes
Agencies/regulatory groups	Phone, fax, personal visits, e-mail	
Attending physicians, department chairs, medical director	Phone, fax, personal visits, e-mail, letters, bulletin boards	
Board members	Phone, fax, letters, e-mail	
Clergy	Phone, e-mail	
Community groups	Phone, fax, personal visits, e-mail	
Community opinion leaders	Phone, fax, personal visits, e-mail	
Donors	Letters, fax, e-mail	
Elected officials	Phone, fax, personal visits, e-mail, special briefings	
Employees/management	Bulletin boards, meetings, group voice mail, e-mail	
General public	Press releases/briefings, media appearances, web page	
Large employers/employer groups	Phone, fax, personal visits, e-mail	
Managed care organizations	Phone, fax, personal visits, e-mail	
Media	Phone, fax, personal visits, e-mail, prepared statements, backgrounders, fact sheets, Q & A, editorial meetings, op-ed, news releases, news conferences, CD-ROM	
Organization's retirees	Letters	
Other healthcare facilities	Phone, fax, e-mail	
Police/fire/emergency personnel	Phone, fax, e-mail	
Prospective employees/recruits	Phone, e-mail	
Referring discharge planners	Phone, fax, personal visits, e-mail	
Referring long-term care providers	Phone, fax, personal visits, e-mail	
Shareholders/bondholders	Prepared statements, e-mail	
Unions	Phone, e-mail	
Volunteers	Volunteer newsletter, face-to-face	

Communications Channels for Other Audiences

Thinking about the audiences you want to reach leads you directly to the next decision: how will you reach them? There are many options, ranging from personal telephone calls and group voice mail to e-mail and website postings. Figure 2-2 is a good place to begin sorting through potential crisis communications audiences and vehicles. Use the "notes" column for organization-specific information that will facilitate the development of a customized communications plan.

Each communications channel has advantages and disadvantages.

- The **telephone** has long been a staple of crisis communications, especially for media inquiries. But the telephone should be used judiciously in a crisis. Incoming media calls in a high-profile crisis can easily overwhelm the organization's capacity to respond. The telephone can be leveraged to full advantage by setting up toll-free numbers dedicated to crisis information. These ad hoc crisis hotlines may be staffed or may offer recorded information that is updated on a regular basis. Consult with telecommunications management to find out how to implement systems like these in your organization.

- **Voice mail** offers another way to use the phone as a tool. Individual voice mail is, of course, indispensable. A word of caution, however; because voice mail precludes two-way communication, messages can sometimes be confusing, incomplete or subject to misinterpretation. This can be particularly frustrating or upsetting to message recipients in a crisis situation. No matter how rushed you feel, be sure to speak slowly and clearly and leave information about how the recipient can reach you for follow-up. If your telephone system has the capacity for creating "all-staff" or departmental voice mail messages, learn how to use this feature *before* you need it.

- **News conferences** provide an efficient way of answering media questions in high-profile crises. In a crisis that is expected to be of long duration, regularly scheduled news conferences can significantly reduce the volume of media calls. In many cases, however, one-on-one briefings may be preferable to a full-scale news conference. (*See Section 3.5 for more information about news conferences.*)

- **E-mail** offers many advantages as a crisis communications tool, particularly in nonmedical crises such as labor disputes or regulatory/accreditation-related investigations. E-mail allows you to go into detail and to maintain control over your "main messages." (*See Section 2.3 for more about developing main messages.*) However, in many hospitals, not everyone has access to e-mail.

- When you want the audience to know how important they are to you, **personal visits** have the edge over e-mail and phone calls. In situations where the organization's image or key relationships are threatened, consider visiting elected officials and representatives of community groups and/or insurers to get your messages across.

- In recent years, **fax** has become secondary to e-mail or voice mail in many cases, a useful backup when those media are unavailable.

USING INTRANETS FOR CRISIS COMMUNICATIONS: RED LIGHT, GREEN LIGHT, YELLOW LIGHT . . . STOP!

At Memorial Health in Savannah, GA, the corporate intranet always lists a "MemCom" status (short for Memorial Communications) of green, yellow or red. Code green means that the organization is operating as normal. Code yellow designates a heightened disaster alert, but the disaster plan has not yet been activated. Once the disaster plan has been activated, MemCom status moves to code red.

The MemCom status indicator clicks through to a dedicated disaster page that provides informational updates, listings of various disaster teams, emergency preparedness plans and more. For instance, during hurricane season, the color-coded status symbol clicks through to hurricane tracking information, weather forecasts and other special alerts.

Memorial Health's MemCom system is also used to notify staff of recall status in the event of a weather-related hospital evacuation. Employees can access MemCom remotely in a variety of ways: by direct-dial computer connection, by accessing a hidden mirror site on the organization's web page at www.memorialhealth.com, by hot-synching their personal digital assistant (PDA) handheld devices such as Palm Pilots, or by wireless web browsing using that same PDA or a cell phone's web browser.

Source: S. Regan, Using Technology to Enhance Crisis Communications. *Spectrum* (Nov. 2001): 6-7.

- **Intranets** present an often untapped resource for crisis communications. A "crisis monitor" on your corporate intranet offers a method for easily alerting employees of the organization's crisis status. Such monitors are particularly useful if your hospital must frequently deal with weather-related emergencies, but they can also be used to alert management and staff of emergency room diversion status, bed availability and other emergency situations, such as mass casualties that are being transported to the hospital.

- An American Hospital Association (AHA) study found that approximately 58 percent of hospitals had websites in 2000 (AHA 2001). But only a fraction of those sites can be used for communicating during a crisis, primarily because of design and staffing limitations that would preclude frequent, real-time updates. Figure 2-3 provides a checklist of issues that must be addressed before your website will be crisis-ready. Hospitals and health systems that are not prepared to use their website during a crisis are missing out on important opportunities for communicating with many of their important audiences as well as reducing the all-important "chaos factor." In times of crisis, your website can:

  - Present and maintain accurate information about the organization.
  - Serve as a rich source of background information.
  - Provide timely, accurate, up-to-date information about the crisis at hand to all audiences, including employees.
  - Facilitate the work of the media.
  - Reduce the number of repeat calls from reporters.
  - Manage negative publicity by stopping the rumor mill in its tracks.
  - Eliminate the time zone issue.

For an example of how a hospital used its website as a primary communications vehicle during a crisis, see Case Study 3.3, *The CEO as Spokesperson in the Matthew Shepard Case.*

- **CD-ROMs** that are used for routine media relations can also be distributed to the media during a crisis. They provide a convenient and relatively inexpensive way to disseminate back-grounders, electronic "media kits," photo archives and media policies and procedures. CDs that are used for this purpose should be updated every year.

FIGURE 2-3
CRISIS READINESS CHECKLIST FOR WEBSITES

This checklist will help you identify issues that must be addressed before your website is crisis-ready.

✓ Make sure that your Internet Service Provider (ISP) can handle the additional traffic your site will experience during a crisis.

✓ Meet with the personnel who can make changes to your site "on the fly." Develop a call schedule so that one of these staffers is always available. As an alternative, consider training public relations or marketing staff to handle this.

✓ Establish a structure for posting press releases and other statements on the website. Eventually, you may wish to consider providing live Internet coverage of media and family briefings.

✓ Decide whether you will accept inquiries about patient conditions via e-mail. If so, accountabilities need to be assigned, parameters need to be developed and compliance with the Health Insurance Portability and Accountability Act of 1996 (HIPAA) needs to be addressed.

✓ Once policies and procedures for web-based crisis communications have been drafted, have your attorneys review them to ensure they meet patient confidentiality and privacy requirements, including HIPAA.

✓ Consider using a "ghost page" or "dark site," a hidden page on your site that is only accessible to those who provide the proper identification/authorization information. This can be useful for providing infor-mation to targeted audiences such as the media, employees or physicians. As an alternative, intranets may be easier to modify and may provide a more secure vehicle for reaching internal audiences.

✓ Before a crisis hits, explore possibilities for linking with other organizations that are actively involved with responding to or reporting on the crisis, such as other area hospitals, the Red Cross and newspapers.

✓ Be sure that the media have your website and e-mail addresses—and that you have theirs.

As an overall communications management tool, **handheld devices**, also known as PDAs or personal digital assistants (think *Palm Pilot*), are growing increasingly popular. They can replace paper-based appointment books, telephone/address books and other work management tools. Handheld devices may be a useful adjunct to your crisis communications toolbox *if* you are well-versed in their use and you are willing to keep them up-to-date. They offer a compact way to store organizational contact lists, media lists and community and governmental contact lists as well as an electronic version of the crisis communications plan. PDAs also come in handy for maintaining a message log during a crisis. If you do use PDAs for a message log or any other purpose during a crisis, periodically upload to your computer network to ensure that no data are lost should you misplace the PDA. Avoid storing confidential patient information on PDAs.

Finally, keep in mind that during some crises, phone service and/or electricity may be down. This means you may not have access to voice mail, computers, e-mail, printers, fax machines or photocopiers. Weather-related disasters are not the only crises that can jeopardize communications. In the event of a "cybersecurity" problem, management may decide to take the organization's intranet offline or suspend e-mail service. Backup plans must be in place for all of these contingencies. No matter how advanced our communications technologies become, there will always be a role for old-fashioned media such as bulletin boards, all-staff briefings and conference room walls that double as message centers.

2.3. GUIDELINES FOR DEVELOPING YOUR MAIN MESSAGES

Messages for Internal Crises

Think about the television commercials that stand out in your mind—that make you laugh or even make you cry—that actually get you thinking about the product or service being advertised. One of the reasons those commercials are effective is because they have one "main message" to convey. There is no long list of product features, no attempt to lay claim to all the superlatives at once. For the viewers, there is no information overload and no confusion—they "get it."

Crisis communications is not unlike advertising in that respect: you must choose the main messages that you want to convey and stay focused on those messages. The number of messages should be limited to three or four key points that are memorable, quotable and brief. More is *not* better in this case. Sometimes it helps to "think in headlines." Choosing your messages carefully is pivotal. Everything else you do will be in support of these messages. As the public relations professional in the organization, you are the primary architect of the main messages. The way you communicate your messages in a crisis situation has a huge impact on how effectively your organization is perceived to be managing the situation.

Crisis messages often serve the following purposes:

- *Convey concern, care and empathy.* When people are upset, they want to know that you care before they can genuinely care about what you know. When appropriate, sincere expressions of sympathy and regret help demonstrate to the media and key stakeholders that your organization regrets what happened and is willing to work with the appropriate authorities to expeditiously resolve the situation. Empathy also goes a long way toward enhancing trust and credibility.

- *Present the known facts, reassure the audience that the situation is under control and describe steps that are being taken to address it.* Be as open and transparent with the media and key audiences as possible. Tell the truth. Embracing an open communications philosophy and providing regular information updates build trust. It also helps your organization gain respect and credibility while representing it in the best possible light and enabling you to frame developments in your organization's favor.

- *Outline actions that are being planned to prevent a recurrence.* This sends a message that your organization is taking ownership of the situation. Particularly in cases where your organization is accused of wrongdoing, quickly outline a proactive plan of action to the media. This will help your organization sustain or regain public trust. Action steps might include the establishment of an independent expert panel to review the situation or the launch of an audit or a redesign of key processes that may have contributed to the problem at hand.

- *Reinforce the organization's commitment to its employees, patients, community and other constituencies.* This is often the last message that is presented. It ends the communication on a positive note and puts the incident in perspective.

In a crisis that does not involve a mass-casualty disaster, the crisis team's first order of business is often to develop main messages. The team will find it helpful to discuss similarities and differences between the current situation and previous crises as well as anticipated target audience reactions. Team members may find it useful to seek input from colleagues who are not on the team before participating in this process. In some cases, legal counsel should approve the statements that are developed based on these main messages. The chief communications executive, as the team leader, is ultimately the architect of the key messages and the arbiter in cases where team members may disagree.

The case studies in this book offer a number of examples of developing main messages in difficult situations. When a patient was shot to death in a gang-related incident in the intensive care unit of Mount Carmel Mercy Hospital in Detroit, the hospital's public relations director developed the following main messages:

- This was an isolated incident. No one else was harmed. (*Presents the facts and reassures the audience.*)
- The nursing staff responded professionally and has been reassuring patients. (*Describes steps that are being taken to address the situation.*)

- Mount Carmel Mercy Hospital is a safe place. Nothing like this has ever happened in its 50-year history. *(Reinforces the organization's commitment to its constituencies.)*
- We are reviewing our policies and procedures to see if any changes are needed in light of this incident. *(Outlines actions that are being planned to prevent a recurrence.)*

See Case Study 2.1, *Shooting in the ICU*, for more information.

In Case Study 2.2, *FBI Raid Launches Fraud and Abuse Investigation*, the chief communications officer for a large managed care organization developed key messages that helped keep system operations running smoothly during a time of intense public scrutiny.

When it was discovered that a number of patients in a community hospital had received insulin injections even though no physician had ordered them, resulting in potentially dangerous episodes of low blood sugar, the hospital's communications director developed the following main messages:

- The events were discovered through the hospital's internal processes. *(Reassures the audience.)*
- The hospital followed all protocols and reported the events to the appropriate agencies. *(Describes steps that are being taken to address the situation.)*
- Patient confidentiality prevents the hospital from commenting on the specifics. *(Presents the facts. Sometimes, patient confidentiality concerns will limit the facts that can be disclosed.)*
- The hospital's top priority was—and remains—ensuring the safety of its patients and employees. *(Reinforces the organization's commitment to its constituencies.)*

See Case Study 4.2, *Unexplained Medical Findings*, for more information.

Messages for Mass Casualty Crises and High-Profile Medical Emergencies

In crises that involve medical emergencies, the focus of crisis messages is often very simple: how many patients are being treated at the hospital, who they are and what condition they are in. The key to providing this information is creating a patient log with information about all individuals who are treated in the hospital emergency department.

The log should include space for the following information:
- Arrival time
- Name, age and gender
- City of residence
- Admitting diagnosis
- Patient condition
- Condition updates over a period of hours or days
- Room number
- Location updates as the patient is transferred from emergency room to intensive care to medical-surgical unit, etc.

- A checkbox to indicate whether next-of-kin has been notified
- Name and phone number of next-of-kin
- Final disposition
- Medical record number

Without prior patient authorization, only the patient's name and one-word condition should be released to the media. The other information you collect will be useful when responding to inquiries from family members and coordinating patient rosters with rescue workers and other hospitals that received patients from the disaster.

In 2001, the Society revised the *Guidelines for Releasing Information on the Condition of Patients,* which is reprinted in its entirety in Appendix B. Multiple copies in a convenient brochure format may be ordered from the AHA online store at www.ahaonlinestore.com.

The *Guidelines* were revised and updated in 2001 to be consistent with HIPAA privacy regulations. Highlights of the *Guidelines* include the following:

- Media inquiries must contain the patient's name.

- You may release only the patient's one-word condition and location without obtaining prior patient authorization. For the one-word condition, use the terms "undetermined," "good," "fair," "serious" or "critical."

- As a matter of policy, the patient's location in the hospital should not routinely be given to the media. Be sure that security personnel are aware of this policy. The patient's location is included in the hospital directory to facilitate visits by friends and family as well as the delivery of flowers and gifts.

- Detailed statements about patients, photographs of patients or interviews with patients all require written authorization from the patient.

- Patients can "opt out" of providing information altogether.

- Do not release any information that could embarrass or endanger patients.

- Celebrities, as well as patients who are involved in matters of public record, have the same privacy rights as all other patients, as far as the hospital is concerned.

- HIPAA does not preclude hospitals from sharing patient information with other hospitals, healthcare facilities and rescue/relief agencies in disaster situations.

Some of these recommendations represent a significant change from previous hospital practices. In particular, limiting the information released to the patient's name and one-word condition may be a major change. It may be helpful to proactively provide the media with a copy of the Society's *Guidelines* or your hospital's policies *in advance* of any crisis to validate the regulatory basis for these new policies.

There are other messages you may want to convey in a mass casualty disaster as well. These include appeals to the community for blood donation, instructions to employees (when phone service and other communications channels have been disrupted) and information about disaster-related services that are available—or unavailable—at the hospital.

In a medical emergency that involves celebrities or victims of high-profile crimes or accidents, you will often want to speak for the patients and their families—to convey their wish for privacy or their thanks for the public's support, for example. In some cases, you may wish to publish an address to which cards and gifts may be sent or instructions for donating to a fund for a patient's benefit or in a patient's memory. Or you may want to establish an e-mail or website address where well-wishers can send messages.

Whenever a media request for a patient interview is received, communications professionals should counsel the patient about the positive and negative consequences of giving information to the media. Often, patients and their families who are initially apprehensive about releasing information will develop a comfort level with the process once they understand the potential benefits.

Of course, some patients genuinely want to avoid publicity and media contact; it is your responsibility as the hospital's communications professional to see that their wishes are respected. Case Study 2.3, *A Hate Crime Against Children*, tells of a situation where a hospital successfully protected a family's privacy after a shooting that drew international media attention.

2.4. THE WORDS TO SAY IT: FINDING YOUR VOICE

Words are very powerful tools. Used well, they can communicate a sense of control, efficiency and order. When blended with relevant, verified facts, the right choice of words can help mitigate nearly any bad situation. When crafting your response to a crisis, particularly one that focuses on the organization's deeds (or misdeeds), consider the following tips. Additional guidelines for communicating about such incidents with internal audiences are provided in Chapter 4.

- Avoid using "negative" and "absolute" language.
  Find alternatives to saying "no," "not," "never, "nothing" or "none." Negatives can create an impression that you are defensive, arrogant or combative. It is easy to discredit a messenger delivering absolute messages. In addition, absolute messages make it difficult to present alternative options for addressing the situation.

- **Avoid speculation.**
  Speculating about things that are not yet known or are out of your domain is almost always coun-
  terproductive and potentially problematic. Therefore:
  ✓ Avoid making premature dollar estimates of property damage.
  ✓ Avoid making premature assessments of an individual's or organization's performance.
  ✓ Do not speculate about another party's reactions or opinions; refer such questions to that
    organization or individual.
  ✓ Do not assign blame or argue legalities.
  ✓ Avoid speculating about hypothetical situations. There are an endless number of possible
    scenarios, ranging from negative to nightmarish, most of which will never come to pass.
    Focus on the situation at hand.

- **Focus on what your audience is truly concerned about.**
  When discussing the impact of a crisis on your organization's **operations**, emphasize that safety
  (of patients, employees or other affected groups) is a top priority. Make it clear that your organization will take full responsibility for ensuring that alternative arrangements are made for anyone
  who is affected by an interruption in service.

  When discussing **security** issues, stress the precautions your organization is taking to ensure the
  safety of all involved. Also discuss the steps you are taking to prevent similar problems in the future.

  When responding to **controversies**, stress the anticipated community benefits of your organization's position and use factual data to support the idea that your organization has the public interest at heart.

- **Be sure that your key messages are clear, concise and free of ambiguity and jargon.**
  If your audience does not understand your message, you could make a difficult situation worse
  rather than better. Think about the audience's perspective and frame your message in language
  they will understand.

- **When appropriate, use credible third-party sources to speak on your organization's behalf.**
  Identifying people outside your organization with expertise related to the issue at hand can provide an objective and credible perspective. When negative messages are coming from outside your
  organization, having a different third-party source counter that point of view can be far more
  effective than anything your organization can do. Third-party experts can advocate on your behalf
  or offer supporting evidence that could help enhance your organization's credibility.

- **Ensure that your responses are consistent over time and among spokespeople being interviewed.**
  Coordinated delivery of messages ensures not only consistency, but also a uniform tone, which
  can have a significant impact on how the public receives your organization's message.
  Occasionally, a patient engages a public relations representative and/or an attorney who wish to
  make a statement on the patient's behalf. (*See Case Study 2.4*, Trauma at a Laundromat, *for an
  example.*) Managing communications in this situation can be a challenge. It is preferable to avoid

holding joint news conferences with patients' private representatives because the audience may be confused about who is speaking for the hospital or health system. If there is no alternative, find out exactly what these individuals intend to say before any media encounter. In the event of a disagreement about the information that should or should not be released, it may be necessary to limit releasable information to a minimum and compel the patients' private representatives to find another forum. Your legal or risk management counsel can advise you further.

Case Study 2.5, *When Patient Safety Is Called into Question*, exemplifies the development of appropriate main messages in a difficult situation.

2.5. WHEN TO RELEASE INFORMATION

Maximum disclosure with minimum delay is almost always the best strategy.

- **Tell internal audiences first.** Employees, physicians, board members and others should not hear bad news from the media first. It will be easier to hear if it comes from you. If you find out that the media is releasing information before you thought they would, assemble the troops and break the news as fast as you can, even if you do not have all the i's dotted and the t's crossed.

- **Anticipate and prepare for key events that could trigger media interest.** Prepare media strategies and communications materials in advance. You can then respond to media inquiries promptly and effectively, avoiding the "no comment" sound bite. Saying "no comment" almost always carries a negative connotation.

- **Strategize about the merits of proactive news releases or media interviews versus reactive media statements.** In some situations, chances are good that a crisis will not generate media interest unless a third party intervenes to stimulate interest or other unforeseen events occur. In this situation, if the organization wants to avoid publicity, it may make sense to prepare messages and statements in case media inquiries come in rather than proactively issuing news releases. But if the crisis is such that media attention is inevitable—it's just a matter of time—a proactive approach will be to your advantage. Don't wait for the proverbial shoe to drop. At the same time, realize that there are many factors to take into account when timing the initial release of information. You will need to balance organizational readiness factors with the situation-specific risks and benefits of releasing information at a given time.

- **Act quickly and responsively.** Once a decision is made to proactively release information, disseminate it as soon as possible to diminish negative speculation. Be aware of and respect media deadlines. If senior management or legal counsel must approve statements before they are released to the media, streamline these organizational processes to facilitate a quick response. Delays in responding can lead to perceptions of stonewalling.

- **In the case of crimes when someone is accused of deliberate wrongdoing, timing is critical.** Address the alleged crime too late, and your crisis communications plan will suddenly become a defensive strategy—and one that will be difficult to convert to offense. On the other hand, if you address the alleged crime too soon, you may open yourself up to litigation and castigation. It is usually best to assume that information will find its way to the media—one way or another—*before* you are prepared to release it, and to be prepared for that scenario.

- **If a reporter catches you off guard, do not panic.** Ideally, the first information the media receives about a situation should come from the organization's communications professionals. Your personal communications reputation and the stature of your organization will benefit from this straightforward, direct approach. And this proactive strategy gives you control of the situation. Inevitably, though, there will be times when a reporter's request for reaction to a story is the first you have heard of it. This situation is always unsettling—you are being asked to respond to something you know absolutely nothing about.

In such cases, be straightforward: "This is the first I've heard about it. Let me find out what is happening and call you back." Then do just that: take the reporter's name, the name of the media outlet and the deadline, find out what is going on, initiate your crisis communications plan (if the situation requires it) and respond. (*See Section 3.6 for more information about media statements.*)

The classic example of a healthcare crisis that was expertly handled is the tainted Tylenol tragedy in 1982. Seven people died in the Chicago area after taking Tylenol capsules that had been laced with cyanide, setting off a national panic. The crime has yet to be solved. Johnson & Johnson saved its reputation and its most profitable product by its adept handling of the crisis. The company acted quickly to recall and destroy all 31 million bottles of the largest-selling over-the-counter medicine in the country. Six weeks later, it introduced a Tylenol package with a tamper-resistant seal.

Johnson & Johnson's crisis communications plan emphasized protecting public interest and used the media to spread its message. The J & J spokesperson described the company's strict quality control measures and informed the media of the tainted capsules' lot numbers and the plants from which they had been shipped. The spokesperson left it to government authorities to comment that the tampering must have occurred after the capsules reached Illinois; although the spokesperson might have known this, it was out of his purview and therefore more credible coming from a third party (Herman 2002). J & J chief executive Jim Burke appeared on TV shows such as *Phil Donahue* and *60 Minutes*, taking ownership of the situation, expressing the company's concern for the victims and pledging to find ways to prevent product-tampering in the future. Handled less skillfully, this crisis could very well have spelled the end for Tylenol. Instead, the brand emerged stronger and the company ushered in a new era of tamper-resistant packaging for over-the-counter medication.

CASE STUDY 2.1
SHOOTING IN THE ICU

At approximately 5:30 p.m. on a September Monday, Rose Glenn, director of marketing and public relations at Mount Carmel Mercy Hospital in Detroit, heard the hospital's trauma team being paged to a nursing unit. She scarcely had time to wonder why the team was going to a nursing unit instead of the emergency room before the phone rang.

It was the local CBS network affiliate saying they had received a call from a patient reporting that the patient next door had just "gotten blown away."

When Glenn arrived on the unit, she confirmed that a patient had indeed been shot in the head—in fact, she and Mount Carmel's CEO LeRoy Fahle looked on as the patient was declared dead. Fahle turned to Glenn and asked, "What are we going to say?"

The hospital's first priority was to make sure no other patients were in danger. They found out from the nursing staff that the suspect fled down the stairs and out of the building—thus, no other patients were at risk. The gunman apparently had targeted only one patient, shot him and escaped.

Glenn knew two other things critical to crisis management: the evening news programs would cover the story and patients would be viewing the reports. She suggested that the CEO and the nursing administrator visit all the patients in the wing of the hospital where the shooting took place and reassure them of their safety.

Meanwhile, Glenn served as spokesperson. Her main messages were as follows:
- This was an isolated incident. No one else was harmed.
- The nursing staff responded professionally and were themselves reassuring patients.
- Mount Carmel Mercy Hospital is a safe place. Nothing like this had ever happened in its 50-year history.

Questions about metal detectors added a fourth message when needed: "We're reviewing our policies and procedures to see if any changes are needed in light of this incident." (Subsequently a decision was made *not* to install metal detectors.)

Glenn wanted every patient, doctor, board member and employee (on all shifts) to be kept well-informed. She and another member of the public relations staff delivered letters to all nursing units, the doctors' lounge and the dining room. The letters addressed the three main message points and added information that the patient had originally come to the hospital with a gunshot wound and "police believe the two incidents are related." The letter emphasized that the safety of patients, employees and visitors is of "utmost concern" to the hospital.

No one panicked. There were no requests for transfers out of the hospital, and only one request for a transfer to another floor.

Glenn handled all media inquiries over the next two days. The daily newspaper did an investigative piece revealing that the victim had been a drug kingpin and was apparently shot for drug-related reasons. Because his original admission was for gunshot wounds, the police speculated that "an alleged hit man" had "failed to complete his job."

The incident generated more media attention than any other story in Glenn's seventeen-year career. She focused her communications on the three or four main messages. All other questions were referred to the police. She refrained from speculating about the victim's background or the reasons for the shooting.

Mount Carmel Mercy Hospital already had a policy to protect victims of violent crime. The "No I" or "no information" policy automatically applied when anyone was admitted for treatment of a gunshot or a stabbing wound. The policy prohibited guests from visiting and precludes any information—including confirmation of the patient's presence—from being released to anyone. Only the patient could remove the "No I" order. The victim had, in fact, lifted the "No I" order just hours before he was killed. And the assassin had duly obtained a visitor's pass before making his way to the ICU.

LESSONS LEARNED

- Every hospital needs a policy that seeks to protect patients, such as crime victims, who may be at risk of attack by individuals who would enter the hospital for that purpose.

- The ability to formulate key messages quickly is crucial. In some cases, you will literally be thinking on your feet as a crisis unfolds around you.

- Personal contact is especially important in situations where patients may be worried about their safety. Once you are certain that patients and employees are safe, enlist senior management to spread the word. Make sure they understand what the key messages are.

- Put the incident in perspective. By using phrases such as "isolated incident" and "first such incident in the hospital's 50-year history," Mount Carmel effectively conveyed the message that the hospital was a safe place.

- Do not deviate from your key messages. Avoid speculating about events that are beyond the scope of your organization's involvement in an incident, including events that led up to a patient's admission to the hospital, or the patient's life outside the hospital. However, if authorities have made statements about the crisis victim(s) or perpetrator(s) that affect the actual or perceived risk to other patients or employees, these statements should be used or at least addressed in your crisis communications messages.

CASE STUDY 2.2
FBI RAID LAUNCHES FRAUD AND ABUSE INVESTIGATION

It was just another July day at the corporate headquarters of Columbia HCA's North Florida Division—until 18 FBI agents entered the room and herded 12 staffers, including five secretaries, into the boardroom where they would spend the rest of the day. Many of them were intimidated and bewildered by the seemingly inexplicable turn of events.

The FBI advised the employees that if they did not cooperate with the investigation, they could each be arrested for obstruction of justice. They were not to throw anything away. Their phones had been tapped and anyone who wanted to make photocopies of any documents would have to be supervised by an FBI agent.

What the corporate staff didn't know was that, at the same time, more than two-dozen Columbia offices were also being raided.

Marty Campanello, then the division's chief marketing and communications officer, soon was in the fray. His first priority: the employees. He provided the staff with a set of hastily prepared but cogent talking points. He also reminded them that their mission of providing high-quality healthcare to their patients had not changed.

Next, he turned his attention to managing the media. The building was sealed off, using internal security staff, to avoid any unwanted photo opportunities. No interviews were given to the media; instead, the division issued a press release that emphasized the following:

- Columbia HCA, like the government, believed there should be a crackdown on fraud.
- Columbia hoped to be presumed innocent and to be given its day in court.
- Columbia would not be diverted from providing the highest quality healthcare to the thousands of people who used their services every day.

Over the course of the next three days, FBI agents searched each staff person's desk and the central files, piece by piece. By the time the search was over, agents had removed 82 large boxes full of files; most of them could not be photocopied. Columbia's attorneys were present during much of this process, observing and answering questions.

Even while the FBI was still on site, a series of e-mail messages was sent to managed care contractors and other key audiences, reiterating Columbia's three key message points.

And when the agents finally left, the communications team began working with physicians, board members, volunteers and legislators. "Blast" faxes, telephone calls and personal visits were the primary communications media. Much attention was also given to the employees. They were provided with talking points for use with their friends, families and neighbors.

The division arranged conference calls with other Columbia divisions to share media experiences and strategies. Daily conference calls were also set up with national corporate management to keep them informed of all developments.

Within two weeks, an image-rebuilding plan was developed and implemented. Research revealed that people were more concerned about care at the local level than about any goings-on with the FBI. There was a notable exception: seniors who wanted to make sure that Columbia wasn't cheating Medicare. A "don't-be-alarmed" letter was sent to patients. That letter, along with talking points developed for physicians and nurses, was very effective—patient volume losses were minimal and short-lived.

In the weeks that followed, the division noted some negative effect on employee recruitment but not on retention. To put things in their proper perspective, employees were urged to look at the care Columbia hospitals provided in emergency services and newborn nurseries. Doing so helped employees see for themselves that the FBI action was not a quality issue.

LESSONS LEARNED

- The system would have been better prepared had this type of situation been addressed in its crisis communications plan. Just because FBI raids and other "legal emergencies" are rare happenings, do not forget to include these scenarios in your planning.

- Do not forget your internal audiences, including employees, physicians and staff.

- Keep your perspective: "You will survive."

- Include the hospital attorneys' telephone numbers on your emergency phone number list.

CASE STUDY 2.2

CASE STUDY 2.3
A HATE CRIME AGAINST CHILDREN

On August 10, 1999, at about 11 a.m., a self-proclaimed neo-Nazi gunman went on a shooting rampage in the North Valley Jewish Community Center in Granada Hills, CA. Three children, a teenage girl and an elderly woman were shot.

Two children were brought to Childrens Hospital Los Angeles (CHLA): One sustained bullet wounds to the lower back and leg; the other, the most seriously injured of the five victims, suffered bullet wounds to the abdomen and leg. The second child had initially been taken to another hospital and was then transferred to CHLA after his condition was stabilized at about 11:30 p.m.

The media calls went on all night long. Of the 35 calls that manager of external communications Steve Rutledge took between midnight and 6 a.m., many were from the East Coast and the major networks, including CNN and MSNBC. But calls also came from as far away as Israel.

After a sleepless night, Rutledge arrived at the hospital to find three satellite trucks waiting. (He had some advance warning; security officers had paged him.) Rutledge quickly determined that a situation of this magnitude required full implementation of the hospital's crisis communications plan. CHLA uses the Hospital Emergency Incident Command System (HEICS)* as the basis for its crisis communication plan.

Three public relations staff members and three surgeons quickly responded to media interviews. Just as quickly, the engineering staff started laying cable in a lecture hall designated to serve as the media communications center during disasters.

A news conference was called; Rutledge began by reading a letter from the parents of the first boy thanking people for their good wishes and asking the media to respect their privacy.

The hospital also used the opportunity to issue a plea for blood donors. Blood was in short supply during August (a result of summer vacations) and the response was immediate. Later, 32 news media outlets covered the first boy's release from the hospital, with photo opportunities galore as he waved and left.

The other injured child continued to be treated for several weeks. Throughout the treatment, media calls continued to come in. Interviews were requested by media outlets ranging from *People* magazine and the *Today Show* to the local newspaper.

Government officials and religious leaders called asking to visit the child; even a faith healer called to offer help. All calls were forwarded to Rutledge and logged in as they were received. Twice each day, the messages were given to the boy's parents who remained adamant in their wish to avoid media contact. As an added safeguard, the parents were permitted to park inside the hospital's emergency entrance to avoid unwanted media contact.

Rutledge did everything he could to protect the young patient's privacy. He explained to reporters that the boy's family's primary concern was for his health and that they would talk with the media *after* he went home from the hospital.

The parents remained at their son's bedside while CHLA's medical spokespersons made appearances on *Good Morning America*, *Today*, *Larry King Live* and other news magazine format shows. Rutledge briefed the doctors on what they could—and could not—say. He also found diplomatic ways to advise a physician with a heavy accent how to speak slowly and distinctly.

News briefings continued every day during the first week following the shootings. A week after the briefings had begun, Rutledge read a formal statement issued by the boy's parents, expressing their appreciation to well-wishers.

At one point, rumors started swirling that the boy was going to be transferred to another facility because of health insurance requirements. A news release quickly set things straight explaining that the boy would remain at CHLA until he was ready to be discharged.

Note: Many hospitals request a template for a crisis communications plan. Although there is no "one-size-fits-all" template, an example of a comprehensive emergency management system with a crisis communications component is the Hospital Emergency Incident Command System (HEICS), a project of the San Mateo County (CA) Department of Health Services' Emergency Medical Services Agency, with the California Emergency Medical Services Authority. HEICS employs a logical management structure, defined responsibilities, clear reporting channels, and a common nomenclature to help unify hospitals with other emergency responders. The entire plan is available at http://www.emsa.cahwnet.gov/dms2/heics3.htm. A video introduction to HEICS is also available free of charge by sending an e-mail to cheryl.starling@emsa.ca.gov.

LESSONS LEARNED

- No matter how much media attention is focused on a patient, if the patient (or the patient's family) does not want publicity, your first responsibility is to shield him or her from it. Physicians or other spokespeople who meet with the media should understand exactly what information and how much information the patient is comfortable releasing.

- In a high-profile case, the more help you have, the better. CHLA pulled in a dozen people to escort media to the right place, ensure that media stayed out of the pediatric intensive care unit, log phone calls and keep the entire process under control. Whenever there are multiple staff members involved, it is important to ensure that everyone logs media calls with meticulous attention to detail to avoid confusion, misinformation and missed connections.

CASE STUDY 2.3

CASE STUDY 2.4
TRAUMA AT A LAUNDROMAT

Mother's Day, 1997: A four-year-old boy at a Los Angeles laundromat with his mother reaches into a clothes dryer while it is running. The machine fails to stop; the boy's arm is instantly torn off at the elbow. His mother pulls the detached limb out of the dryer and calls 911.

The accident happened at 7 p.m. Surgery at Childrens Hospital Los Angeles (CHLA) went on for more than 12 hours. At 10:30 p.m., an orthopedic surgeon who had completed his part of the delicate surgery talked with reporters in time to provide details for 11 p.m. newscasts.

Within minutes of the accident, Steve Rutledge's pager started going off—so fast he could not write the numbers down. Rutledge, who is manager of external communications for CHLA, knew from experience that the morning would be chaos unless he took control of the situation soon.

During the long surgical procedure, Rutledge kept reporters informed about when surgery was expected to be over. When he arrived at the hospital the next morning, he set up a press briefing for 11:30 a.m.—an efficient and effective means of disseminating information to all media outlets simultaneously. The orthopedic surgeon who had spoken with reporters the previous night, the little boy's parents and the surgical team all met with the media.

By the next day, the child's parents had retained an attorney as well as a public relations consultant. (The family would later win a multimillion-dollar lawsuit.) The parents told Rutledge that all news advisories had to be reviewed—and approved—by both the attorney *and* the consultant.

The dramatic nature of the accident sparked national media attention from outlets such as *Extra* and *Hard Copy*. Requests from these outlets were referred directly to the family's attorney.

Surgeons did several one-on-one interviews with the media in the following days. A month later, when the boy went home, a final news conference was held. The child still comes to CHLA for physical therapy and has regained 75 percent use of his arm.

LESSONS LEARNED

- Recognize media events in the making. If you anticipate strong media interest in a story, start arranging for media communications immediately. Don't wait for the deluge.

- Be prepared to deal with patients' attorneys or others who take an ombudsman role in cases of all types. Having—and following—solid media relations guidelines will help prevent disputes and/or differences of opinion between you and such outside representatives.

- Do not speculate on events that transpired before the patient arrived at the hospital or events that might happen after the patient leaves.

- Consider advance media training for physicians who are likely to be involved in high-profile cases. Media training need not always be done by consultants; public relations staff can provide valuable coaching. By taking on this expert consulting role, public relations staff can not only improve the outcome of the situation at hand, but also enhance the stature of the public relations department.

- Unless the nature of the information in the interview is likely to be of an extremely controversial nature, Rutledge prefers to use articulate doctors or nurses *without* media training because they come across as more believable if they don't seem *too* media savvy.

  If certain questions deal with sensitive issues, the physicians and other spokespersons do rehearse. Rutledge provides "do's and don'ts" for physicians prior to an interview.

  "Little things, like: look at the interviewer, not the camera. . . consider it a conversation with the interviewer but don't say anything you don't want to hear repeated in the news. We also discuss the particulars of the case. Sometimes, there may be information we can't legally release, or that the family doesn't want us to release," said Rutledge.

CASE STUDY 2.4

CASE STUDY 2.5
WHEN PATIENT SAFETY IS CALLED INTO QUESTION

On November 16, 2001, St. Cloud Hospital conducted a press conference to announce that it was working with the Minnesota Department of Health and the Centers for Disease Control and Prevention (CDC) to determine the cause of two patient deaths following knee surgery.

The press conference resulted in coverage on all of the Minneapolis/St. Paul network television affiliates (most including reporter stand-ups in front of the hospital), the front page of St. Cloud's daily newspaper and the metro dailies. Subsequent media attention came from across the United States.

The next day, a patient in another Minnesota community died following knee surgery there.

On November 18, the Minnesota Department of Health issued a directive to suspend all elective knee surgery at hospitals throughout the state after three patients died unexpectedly following knee surgery. Two of those patients had been operated on at St. Cloud Hospital.

St. Cloud decided to go beyond the scope of the health department mandate and suspend all elective orthopedic surgeries, not just knee surgeries. On November 18, the hospital issued a press release that included a statement by St. Cloud president John Frobenius: "We are suspending all elective orthopedic surgeries even though detailed reviews of St. Cloud Hospital's operating rooms and patient care practices have not turned up any factors that could have caused these deaths. We believe our decision is in the best interest of the patients, for their safety and peace of mind." Also included in the press release was information about other steps being taken by the hospital. All patients who had undergone knee surgery in the past two weeks would receive a call from the medical group to provide information, inquire about their condition and answer questions. In addition, a letter would be distributed to all patients and their families explaining the situation and stating that the hospital was cooperating fully with the state health department and the CDC in their investigations.

When an exhaustive investigation by the health department subsequently failed to disclose any links among the three deaths, the knee surgery moratorium was lifted. On November 23, the hospital issued another press release. This follow-up press release featured a prominent quote from an epidemiologist at the Minnesota Department of Health: "St. Cloud Hospital has cooperated with us fully on this investigation, and they have been under very intense scrutiny over the last several days. People who are scheduled to have surgery at this facility can proceed with total confidence in their safety." The release also described other steps the hospital had taken to ensure patients' safety and concluded with a quote from Dr. Daniel

Whitlock, St. Cloud's vice president for medical affairs: "Our deepest sympathy is extended to the families of all three patients. While we continue to follow up on various details of the three cases, our medical leadership believes that it is safe to continue to proceed. The health department has come to a similar conclusion." (At press time, both releases were available online at the St. Cloud Hospital website, www.centracare.com.)

LESSONS LEARNED

St. Cloud, faced with a difficult situation that demanded an immediate reaction, exemplified the guidelines for handling such situations:

- The hospital developed a plan of action and conducted a press conference, followed by press releases as new developments occurred.

- In suspending all orthopedic surgeries rather than just knee surgery, the hospital went beyond what was required to demonstrate its commitment to patient safety.

- The initial press release included a statement from the hospital CEO that emphasized his concern for patients' safety and peace of mind. The statement referred to the favorable results of the hospital's internal review but did not go beyond the scope of what was known at that time.

- A multifaceted communications campaign, including telephone calls to knee surgery patients and letters to all current patients, was launched immediately.

- When the state investigation did not turn up a common source of infection, the follow-up press release quoted a third-party expert—a health department epidemiologist involved in the investigation—to deliver the good news, thereby enhancing credibility.

"We were able to develop and execute an effective communications plan in this tragic situation because of three key factors," said Jeanine Nistler, St. Cloud's director of communications. "The hospital president championed the position that we should be open with the public; the administrative and clinical staffs brought communications into the loop immediately; and we had a well-established, positive relationship with those staffs which allowed us to be trusted and relied upon in this crisis."

CASE STUDY 2.5

MEDIA RELATIONS IN A CRISIS

As described in the previous chapter, the quick and candid release of information during a crisis is almost always in the best interest of your organization and your community. Therefore, you should strive to be responsive to the media while simultaneously protecting patient confidentiality and meeting the needs of patients and their families. This chapter offers guidelines and practical advice for accomplishing just that.

3.1. GUIDELINES FOR INTERACTING WITH THE MEDIA

A crisis does not occur in a media vacuum. When the media come to your hospital in the midst of a crisis, they bring with them their perceptions of the hospital, their expectations about your response to the crisis and their attitudes about how the crisis should be portrayed—all based on their previous interactions with your staff and their knowledge of your organization. Therefore, a prerequisite to effective crisis communications is the development and maintenance of a solid working relationship with the media—in *good* times.

Media interactions run the gamut from routine to extraordinary. Clearly, the unannounced arrival of a crew from *60 Minutes*—lights on, cameras rolling, microphones shoved in your face—presents a different kind of challenge than the reporter from your local radio station who calls for an interview. Nonetheless, there are some guidelines for media relations that will not vary, regardless of the type of crisis or the size of the audience to whom the media are reporting. The media have a right to be treated like the important customers they are, and you have a right to be treated as a valued source of information and knowledge. Concentrate on these fundamentals.

What the Media Should Expect from You

- **Clear ground rules.** Your organization's media access policies and procedures should be readily available, understandable and livable for all parties. (*See Section 3.2 for more information about media access policies.*)

- **Honesty.** Within the bounds of confidentiality and privacy, honesty in media relations, especially during a crisis, is not only the *best* policy, it is the *only* one. If you cannot release any information, instead of saying "no comment" you can say: "It's difficult to comment without all of the facts" or words to that effect. When you cannot provide certain types of information, tell the media just that.

- **Frequent contact.** Do not hide from the media. If they cannot find you, and if they cannot get accurate information from you, they will just find it—or some facsimile of it—somewhere else. Schedule frequent updates via fax, e-mail, Internet postings, news conferences and bulletins. Do not be afraid to call impromptu briefings when you have an update or something significant to report.

- **Creature comforts.** Are you tired? So are the media. Depending on the story, they may be a long way from home, working in unfamiliar territory and under directives sent down from their headquarters. So, anything you can do to make their lives a bit better will be appreciated and may result in balanced—if not just better—coverage. Make sure the media are well supplied with plenty of paper, pens, telephones, fax machines, Internet access—and food. You will be feeding staff, rescue workers and volunteers during many crises—add the media to the list. It is a small expenditure and one that will pay off. (*See Section 3.7 for more information about setting up a media center.*)

- **Technical assistance.** Along with access to authoritative spokespersons, this gesture on your part will produce favorable results. If a television station needs to park its satellite uplink in your parking lot, let them if you can. If a newspaper reporter's computer has broken and she is on deadline and needs to file her story, give her computer access.

- **Access to authoritative spokespersons/experts.** Of all the things you can do to cement your positive relationships with the media during times of crisis (and, for that matter, at all other times, too), making experts available to answer questions is one of the best.

  When President Reagan was shot in 1981, Dr. Dennis O'Leary was thrust onto the national stage and into the national psyche for his adroit handling of the media. His calm, unflappable, direct, honest media briefings were a textbook example of good crisis communications. O'Leary's performance was so outstanding that the predecessor to the AHA's Society for Healthcare Strategy and Market Development—the American Society for Health Care Marketing and Public Relations—conferred lifetime honorary membership status on O'Leary. Until his stint as a media spokesperson, O'Leary was relatively unknown in medical leadership circles. Afterwards, his presence was significant and he was tapped to head the Joint Commission.

- **Uncompromising integrity (the "patients and family first" policy).** Although it may not seem like it in the midst of the fray, most members of the fourth estate quite clearly understand that, in times of crisis, they are *not* your highest priority. When human lives are involved, you are responsible for your patients first—and above all else. When the institution's viability and reputation are the source of the crisis, your organization comes first—always. Healthcare communicators who abide by this principle may not make every reporter happy, but quite often the needs of patients and their families, your organization *and* the media can all be well served. Patients and their families come to trust the advice of the communications professional; the media come to respect the communicator and regard him or her as an adjunct resource.

- **A customer service orientation.** The media represent a significant market segment in times of crisis, just as they do at all other times. Thus, one of the most important strategic objectives you can have is to learn what the media need from you to do its job—and deliver, to the best of your ability and within the bounds of propriety and confidentiality, the product (usually information) to the customer (the media).

What You Should Expect from the Media

- **Respect for your organization's media policies and procedures.** All hospitals and health systems should have policies in place that safeguard patient privacy and confidentiality of information. These policies usually spell out the requirements that the media must follow to gain access to patients and the procedures that the hospital has established to facilitate the orderly gathering of information with minimal disruption to patient care and hospital operations. You have a right to expect the media to follow the letter and the spirit of these policies.

- **Honesty.** It goes without saying that the media are expected to be honest and truthful in everything they report.

- **Courtesy.** The inherent urgency of crisis situations can make it difficult to maintain courtesy and civility. Nevertheless, you *can* set limits. A question that is shouted out, interrupting the proceedings, gets lower priority than a politely asked question. A demand will be treated differently than a request. If you model courteous behavior, you are more likely to elicit the same in return.

3.2. MEDIA ACCESS POLICIES AND MEDIA CALL ROUTING PROCEDURES

Media Access Policies

To protect patient privacy and confidentiality, it is important to have policies and procedures that govern media access to healthcare facilities, patients and staff. Involve media representatives in the development of these policies to help ensure their cooperation and buy-in.

All employees should know what to do if a reporter approaches them and starts asking questions or requesting access. Many hospitals establish policies that require media to be escorted by a member of the public relations staff at all times. This helps ensure that no interviews take place without a patient's permission. It is also advisable to have a policy that prohibits the media from taking photographs of patients or patient care areas unless they have express written permission. In a mass casualty disaster, the media frequently want pictures of patients who are awaiting or receiving treatment in the emergency department. It is your responsibility to protect the privacy of patients and their families during this difficult time.

When a Florida hospital was evacuated due to uncontrolled wildfires in the area, the staff formed a human chain around the patients on their gurneys as they were transported from the hospital to the waiting ambulances, to protect them from having unwanted photos taken. (*See Case Study 3.1, Wildfires Force Hospital Evacuation.*) Chances are, you will never have to resort to such measures. But keep in mind that your primary role is to protect patients' privacy and confidentiality. Sample media access policies and procedures are provided in Figures 3-1 and 3-2.

Media Call Routing Procedures

What happens when a media call comes in? How can you ensure that these calls are routed to the public relations or media relations staff in a timely way? It is important for media calls to be routed promptly and correctly. At the same time, you want to ensure that employees outside the communications department will not attempt to answer a reporter's questions or engage the reporter in any discussion unless specifically asked to do so by the communications department. Therefore, proper media call routing procedures should be widely disseminated throughout the organization.

Figure 3-1 provides sample procedures for media call routing when a reporter contacts someone outside the communications department. The same procedures should be followed for every media inquiry to ensure consistency and provide a system for tracking. Adapt these procedures to include and accommodate organization-specific information, including contact names and numbers for the communications staff, and distribute them to all staff.

Conveying Media Policies and Procedures to the Media

The procedures outlined in Figure 3-1 are targeted to internal audiences. You may also wish to proactively communicate your media policies to the media themselves—before a crisis hits. In materials that are developed for the media's use, phrase policies in such a way that their benefits to the media are readily apparent. This customer service orientation enhances cooperation and fosters good working relationships between the media and public relations staff. For example, the following media policies are provided to reporters by The Medical College of Ohio (MCO), a Toledo-based system that includes three teaching hospitals and four medical, nursing and allied health schools.

> Contact the office of marketing and communications when you need a resource for a health-related story. We will get in touch with the appropriate individual(s) and arrange for an interview, photo opportunity or other request. Other staff will refer any media calls they receive to us, so calling us directly will save you time.

> All media representatives must be escorted by a marketing and communications staff member whenever they are on the MCO campus. This policy helps to ensure that the privacy of our staff and patients is respected. It also assures that you avoid delays by not getting lost and it authorizes your presence at MCO.

> Source: *Reporter's Notebook*, The Medical College of Ohio, 2001.

FIGURE 3-1
RECOMMENDED POLICIES AND PROCEDURES FOR
ROUTING MEDIA CALLS AND ALLOWING MEDIA ACCESS

For employees outside the communications or public relations department:

- If you receive a call from the media, take a message that includes the reporter's name, organization and phone number, specific purpose of the call and the reporter's deadline. Advise the reporter that the call will be returned promptly. Do not answer any questions or engage in any other discussion unless you are specifically asked to do so by the communications department.

- Contact the hospital or health system public relations office and relay the information. If you reach staff's voice mail, follow the instructions in the voice mail greeting to have the individual paged or to reach a designated backup staffer.

- If a media request comes after regular business hours, immediately page the communications staff person on call.

- If the caller has requested to speak with a specific individual within the public relations department, immediately relay the request to that individual, who will follow up with the caller.

- All members of the news media, including photographers and camera crews, are prohibited from entering the facility unless escorted by a member of the public relations department or an approved designee. If you see a reporter or photographer attempting to enter without an escort, ask the person(s) to wait in a reception area while you contact public relations. If there is no one available on site, contact the public relations staffer on call. Call for security backup if necessary.

- Photographing, filming or videotaping patients and patient care activities will only be authorized by the public relations department in special cases. The public relations department will obtain all necessary releases and permissions.

Source: adapted from *Media Communications Procedures*, Geisinger Health System, Danville, PA, March 2000.

In addition to these general media policies, it is advisable to have detailed and specific media policies and procedures expressly for disaster situations. Taking the time to develop such policies ensures that you will think through and resolve all the logistical issues ahead of time and reduces the "chaos factor" during an actual crisis. Policies about media access during disasters may be posted on the hospital's website, included in information packets that are provided to reporters when they are covering other stories or distributed on-site during a crisis. These policies should address the following topics;

- Personal identification, including photo identification cards, which media will be required to wear.
- Entrance(s) that media should use when entering the facility.
- Check-in location and procedures.
- Location of the media center.
- Policies on media access to facility areas outside the media center.
- Procedures for asking questions and obtaining information.
- Anticipated schedule for releasing news updates.
- Anticipated availability of information on the hospital's website, through hotlines and other channels.
- Procedures for making and receiving telephone calls, transmitting faxes and accessing e-mail.
- Policies on cell phone usage.
- Availability of food, drinks and restroom facilities.

St. Francis Hospital & Health Centers in Indianapolis has developed extensive policies and procedures that address media issues during a disaster and posted them on the hospital website, www.stfrancishospitals.org. They are reprinted in Figure 3-2.

FIGURE 3-2
SAMPLE DISASTER/CRISIS GUIDELINES FOR THE MEDIA

If a disaster occurs, **patient care is the first priority** at St. Francis Hospital & Health Centers. However, any of your requests or needs will be met as soon as possible. Please familiarize yourself with the following plan:

1. If a disaster situation exists, all members of the media are required to show media identification to gain admittance to St. Francis Hospital or its facilities.

2. Updates will be provided regularly on the Hospital's media section of its website: http://media.stfrancishospitals.org. Background information, photographs and other information for the media are also available on the site.

3. Media personnel are to enter St. Francis Hospital by the main entrance or from the parking garage or parking area. Upon entering the hospital, members of the media are to check in at the main information desk and ask that someone from the community relations department be paged. A community relations representative will escort the media representative to the emergency area or to the media center, if the disaster requires that the media center be opened. Media representatives will be given an identification badge to fill out and wear at all times while on the hospital's premises if they do not have a picture identification badge from their own organization.

4. A news media communications center will be established in the community relations department at Carson Square (telephone 782-7997). This office will be manned by the community relations department staff throughout the disaster or crisis.

FIGURE 3-2
SAMPLE DISASTER/CRISIS GUIDELINES FOR THE MEDIA (CONTINUED)

5. A member of the community relations staff will act as official hospital spokesperson, unless specific medical information is necessary, in which case, a medical spokesperson will be designated by the hospital's administration.

6. The community relations staff will release information in at least 60-minute intervals, or as news occurs. Information will be announced verbally and then distributed to all media personnel in printed form. This information will also be posted on the media section of the hospital's website, http://media.stfrancishospitals.org. If media personnel request information by telephone, information will be released at 60-minute intervals or as it occurs by conference call or by individual calls to the media outlet. Questions from the media will be accepted after the call, and if the answer is not known at that time, the information will be gathered and given during the next conference call or an individualized response will be provided.

7. If the hospital opens its press center, question cards will be circulated for you to write specific requests and questions. The answers will be written on the card and returned to you. If several media personnel ask the same question, the answer will be released during the conference call or briefing.

8. Requests for information or interviews should be made to the community relations staff only. Media representatives who attempt to circumvent the communication process by obtaining unauthorized interviews or by releasing information not confirmed by the community relations staff will politely be asked to leave the media center and the hospital. These individuals, although no longer being granted direct access, may continue to monitor the story through the hospital's website, http://media.stfrancishospitals.org.

9. Community relations will facilitate and coordinate media access to the hospital, administrators, physicians, religious personnel, patients, family and friends during the crisis. We want media to get the story while protecting the privacy of any victims and maintaining uninterrupted medical care. To expedite access and information flow, media personnel will be asked to remain in the disaster media center at all times except for meals and personal necessity unless escorted by a community relations representative to family or victim interviews, etc. Any incoming calls for media will be received by the assigned secretary. A message center will be maintained in this area. Electrical outlets for computers, telephones and private offices will be available for those who need them. Drinks and food will be available in the media center as announced. Restrooms are located near the media center. Cell phones and other wireless technologies have been known to interfere with critical life-saving equipment in hospitals; therefore, general cell phone or wireless technology use within the hospital is restricted. There are designated "safe zones" (including the disaster media center) where cell phones may be used.

10. St. Francis Hospital adheres to the Indiana Hospital Association Guidelines for release of information.

Source: St. Francis Hospital & Health Centers, Indianapolis, IN, www.stfrancishospitals.org.

3.3. Fielding Media Calls

Once a media call is received by the public relations department, how should you proceed? What is involved in responding to a media inquiry? Several steps may be involved, although not every step is needed for every call. Sometimes you have the information at hand and you can answer media questions in real time with no need for a callback. This section outlines procedures for fielding media calls.

- **Create a written record of the media inquiry and include it in the media log.**

  When you receive a call from a reporter, find out who the reporter is, what media outlet he or she represents and what kind of information is being sought. Record this information on a media inquiry form that you have created for this purpose and record it in the media log. (*See Figure 3-3 for a sample media inquiry form.*) This will give you the background information you need to best meet the reporter's information needs. After the call is over, use the notes section of the media inquiry form to record your own impressions of the angle or theme of the interview, any unexpected "tough" questions and messages or themes that seemed to resonate with the reporter.

  During a crisis, this process may need to be abbreviated. If there is time for nothing else, be sure to get the basic contact information. The rest can be added later.

- **Determine who the spokesperson(s) should be and prepare them for the interview.** In many cases, the public relations professional will serve as the spokesperson. If the issues at hand are outside your area of expertise, you will want to find the appropriate experts to serve as co-spokespersons with you or perhaps as the primary spokesperson. Often, it is desirable to have a physician, nurse or other clinician assume this role. For example, during the anthrax exposure incidents in 2001, physicians and public health professionals frequently served as spokespersons. If a crisis involves a public health issue or an unusual or innovative medical procedure or condition, it is advisable to have medical or clinical personnel as spokespersons. If the hospital's practices or procedures are called into question, consider involving an outside expert to lend extra credibility when needed.

  Depending on the CEO's skill and comfort level with the media, the communications professional may suggest that he or she make a statement or take on a larger media communications role. Some communications professionals believe that having the CEO speak lends credibility, demonstrates organizational commitment and provides an element of reassurance in difficult situations. Others hold that the organization is better off if the CEO is kept at a distance from negative events. Decisions about the level of CEO involvement will vary based on organizational culture and customs.

FIGURE 3-3
SAMPLE MEDIA INQUIRY FORM

Date _____

Name of person completing this form _____

About the reporter _____

    Name _____

    Organization _____

    News syndicate affiliations and local distribution (if any) _____

    _____

    Address _____

    City, state, zip _____

    Telephone number_____

    Best time to call _____

    Fax number _____

    E-mail address _____

When would the story run?_____

What types of questions would you like to have answered?_____

_____

_____

If you are not acquainted with the reporter and/or the publication or media outlet, ask the following:

Tell me more about your publication (e.g., scope of distribution, audiences,

frequency of issue) _____

What areas or topics do you usually cover? (e.g., business, healthcare, etc.)

_____

How familiar are you with our organization/product?

_____

_____

Follow-up Items   Date/time promised

_____   _____

_____   _____

_____   _____

Notes

_____

_____

_____

_____

_____

No matter who the spokesperson is, he or she will benefit from knowing what to expect and from being prepared for the interview. (*For information about preparing for and conducting media interviews, see Section 3.4. See Section 4.7 for more information about helping your CEO be a better communicator with internal audiences. See Case Study 3.3, The CEO as Spokesperson in the Matthew Shepard Case, for an example of a situation where the CEO served as a capable spokesperson.*)

- **Develop your main messages and put them in writing**. Written statements may be faxed or e-mailed to reporters. If you use e-mail, the statement should be an attachment to the e-mail message, not in the body of the message. This will help ensure that formatting and other information remain intact. You should have an electronic template with your organization's logo and corporate identity to use for this purpose. (*See Sections 2.3 and 2.4 for information about developing main messages.*)

- **When appropriate, refer the media to outside sources for additional information**. Tell the outside sources about the referral promptly so they will be prepared for a media call.

- **In a crisis where information about patient conditions is needed, release only the appropriate information**. Crises always generate questions about what patient information may be released to the media and when it may be released. (*See Section 2.3 for more information.*)

3.4. EFFECTIVE MEDIA INTERVIEWS

Interviews—whether by telephone or in person—are the cornerstone of media communications. Most well-educated, articulate people believe they can readily handle being interviewed by the news media. After all, they are the experts. Reporters, however, are not necessarily interested in being a conduit for publicizing what you want to say. What they want is to get a story, and sometimes that story is not in line with what you want to convey.

Appearing on local TV newscasts, radio talk shows and in community publications can, however, instantly broaden your reach and enhance your image. Every interview is an opportunity to get you message across.

The key to a successful media interview is confidence. Confidence comes with knowledge. Focus on key topics and preparation. The following tips should assist you in making successful media interviews happen.

Understanding Your Role in the Interview

- Keep in mind that reporters want to communicate accurate, timely information, just as you do.

- Respond promptly to a reporter's call. Remember that the reporter's time constraints are as stringent as your own. Chances are, the reporter is working on other stories besides yours. Respect the reporter's deadline.

- Tell your story. Remember, your side of the story will not be told if you refuse to be interviewed.

- Understand that the media ultimately determine what constitutes news. It is their call, not yours.

- Be as accessible as you can during the entire crisis. If you are hard to find, the reporter may assume that you and the organization are stonewalling.

Before the Interview

- Find out what the interview is about. If you truly understand the topic, you should be able to distill it to a 30-second sound bite. Check your understanding with the reporter. Determine what the reporter needs, the reporter's deadline, the reporter's other contacts within your organization (if any) and the location and estimated length of the interview. If there are some potential areas of sensitivity, such as confidentiality or litigation, find out what you are allowed to release.

- Complete any background work you might require to be fully informed on the topic. If litigation is involved, familiarize yourself with legal terminology that may be applicable to the case.

- Give yourself time to collect your thoughts.

- Radio talk shows often tape interviews over the phone. Just as in any other interview situation, find out the reporter's deadline, set up a convenient time and call him or her back.

- Determine your main messages, focusing on no more than three or four points. Write them down in order of priority. Make sure they are memorable, quotable and brief. Stick to your main messages!

- Practice using the main messages to get the point across.

- Anticipate difficult questions. (*See Figure 3-4 for tips on handling difficult questions.*)

- Practice transitions from negative questions to positive key messages. (*See Figure 3-5 for some examples of language that will help you make those transitions.*)

- Gather supporting facts, statistics and background information. This gives you credibility in the eyes of the audience and makes what you are saying easier to understand. Be prepared to cite sources if questioned. Use statistics that are already public (such as the organization's annual report) if you cannot release certain figures.

- If you are participating in a TV interview, think about ways the reporter can tell your story visually, rather than solely relying on your interview. This might include models, charts or video.

FIGURE 3-4
TOUGH QUESTIONS—AND HOW TO ANSWER THEM

- For the reporter who asks *rephrased questions* repeatedly, give it your best shot two or, at maximum, three times. Then take a page from the best of the Presidential press secretaries and just smile, say you have already answered the question and move on to the next question.

- Any query that begins with *"Isn't it true that ..."* signals a tough question coming up. The minute you hear the phrase and understand the gist of the question, start planning your answer. Need more time? Ask the reporter to repeat the question. A question that begins this way can basically be answered four ways: "Yes." "No." "I don't know." "I'll get back to you when I have more information." Do *not* become defensive—doing so is sure to generate aggressive follow-up questions.

- The *toughest questions of all* are the ones based in truth: "Isn't it true that your organization has been under investigation by the Office of the Inspector General for six months?" The truth is your best defense in such cases. Of course, if you have already told the truth in your press releases and other dealings with the media, then you can easily answer, "No. As I said yesterday ..."

- *"Have you stopped beating your spouse?"* questions are tough to answer, too. ("Isn't it true that the hospital's lack of training for its cath lab technicians is what killed those patients in the cath lab?") Never start by repeating a negative question. (Don't say, "No, it's not true that our lack of technician training killed the patients.") The facts are always a great response: "All of our cath lab technicians are certified by the _____. In addition, we provide each technician with a *minimum* of 50 hours of orientation and training. We are still investigating all the possible causes for the unexplained deaths." Drawing facts into your response is a great way for reporters, and ultimately their readers/viewers, to increase their knowledge of the situation in ways that may make them more favorable to your organization's response to the crisis.

Use tough questions to your advantage. Each question can be used in a FAQ (frequently asked questions) document that can be made available to the public, patients, staff and others via the organization's website. The question may be phrased exactly as it was asked—you have an opportunity to formulate the answer to make your position clear.

- Think about the interview setting. Make sure the place you have chosen is appropriate and relevant to your message. For example, an interview on patient care would best be conducted in a clinical setting. Using a background with the hospital signage or logo is also a good choice. The area should be without clutter, free of interruptions and well lit.

- Check your appearance. Even in print interviews with no camera, appearance is important. Your attire should be clean and neat. Individuals who wear lab coats should remove the pens, note pad and pagers that can weigh down a coat pocket. See Figure 3-6 for suggestions for looking your best on TV.

FIGURE 3-5
HELPFUL INTERVIEW TRANSITIONS

- Let me just add...
- That reminds me...
- Let me answer you by saying that...
- Let me give you some background information...
- Let's take a closer look at...
- That's an important point because...
- What that means is...
- Another thing to remember is...
- Now that you've covered ___, let's move on to ___...
- You may be asking why ___ is true...
- While ___ is certainly important, don't forget that ...
- As I said...
- That's an interesting question. Let me remind you though...
- Before I forget, I want to tell your audience...
- Let me put that into perspective...
- What's important to remember, however, is...
- What I really want to talk to you about is...
- What's most important is...
- And don't forget...
- Before we get off that subject/topic let me add...
- That's not my area of expertise, but what I can tell you is...
- That's a good point, but I think your audience would be interested in knowing that...
- What I'm really here to talk to you about is...

"Lights, Camera, Action:" During the Interview

During the interview, DO:

- Sit forward and straight in your chair. You should appear attentive but relaxed.

- Be assertive and direct. Your message is important.

- Listen carefully to the questions and use your answers to transition or bridge to your message. Back up key points with supporting facts.

Figure 3-6
Tips for Looking Your Best in Television and Videotape Appearances

In a hurricane, flood or earthquake, the last thing you will have time to worry about is how you look. And in times like those, you should not worry about it. It may even be offputting to your audience if you are perfectly groomed while crisis victims are all around you. But if the crisis you are dealing with does not involve a natural disaster and you can prepare ahead of time, then it will help if you look neat, presentable and "TV-ready" so you do not distract from the issue at hand.

- Avoid clothing with large patterns, geometric shapes, tight patterns or pin stripes. Solid colors work best.

- Avoid wearing black, white or red. Even the best cameras have trouble with these colors.

- Be sure that your makeup, wardrobe and hair are consistent with your message.

- Avoid flashy or jangly jewelry.

- Wear your eyeglasses if you want, but tip the bows up slightly off your ears. This angles the lenses down to reduce glare from the lights.

- Wear makeup to reduce the glare of TV lights.

- Bring a handkerchief or tissues to dab perspiration during breaks.

- Do not second-guess the camera. Act as if you are always on screen.

Source: "Public Speaking: Tips for Television, Videotape, and Videoconferencing." Advanced Public Speaking Institute, Landover, MD, www.public-speaking.org.

- Talk to the reporter. Ignore cameras and microphones. Remember that eye contact is critical to TV spokesperson credibility.

- Speak in conversational terms to the public and from the public's point of view. The reporter is the conduit between you and the audience.

- Stress your key messages early and often. State the important facts first, then provide supporting information as time allows.

- Be concise. Speak in sound bites—responses of 20 seconds or less for print or broadcast. Remember that 10-second sound bites are the building blocks of TV news stories. Short, concise excerpts from an interview are key. They help simplify events and explain a story to the audience. Emphasizing your key points more than once will help the reporter choose the most valuable pieces of information.

- Put a face on the story. In some cases, it is helpful to feature a person who has experienced the organization's services firsthand.

- Ask for clarification from the reporter before answering if a question is unclear.

- Correct any misinformation tactfully and do not move on until you are certain the reporter understands.

- Take time to organize your thoughts before speaking or to stop your statement and start over, if needed, during a videotaped interview.

- Remember that the ultimate audience for your words is not the media representative(s) with whom you are speaking. Your audience is their audience.

- Above all, always tell the truth.

Equally important, here are some DON'Ts—behaviors that should be avoided during interviews.

- Don't cross your arms, rock or swivel in your chair or fiddle with desk objects. This makes you appear nervous.

- Don't use complex explanations or industry jargon.

- Don't guess at answers. If for any reason you are unable to answer a question, explain why you do not have an immediate answer. Do not say "no comment." Make a commitment to provide an answer at a later time or to locate the appropriate advisor or spokesperson. Then do it.

- Don't say anything "off the record." There is no such thing. Do not make any statement that you do not want quoted. Avoid offering personal opinions.

- Don't use negative or defensive language.

- Don't make accusations against other organizations, competitors or people.

- Don't be thrown off by interruptions. If the reporter interrupts you in the middle of your sentence, complete your answer before moving on.

- Don't argue with the reporter. Keep your cool.

- Don't let a reporter "put words in your mouth."

- Don't fill voids in the conversation with more information than you have been asked or with idle conversation—no matter how uncomfortable it might seem to remain silent yourself. Silence is a good reporter's best technique.

After the Interview

- Help underscore your message by recommending other people to be interviewed. The more individuals who can reinforce your position and the more background information you can provide, the more likely the reporter will understand your point of view.

- Continue to be as accessible as possible.

- If you committed to provide additional information, be sure to provide the information to the reporter by the agreed-upon time.

If the person who speaks for your organization in time of crisis is someone who is new to the role, you may want to work with him or her in advance so the barrage of questions will not come as a surprise. There are many ways to provide this sort of training. Many public relations and marketing agencies have experience in media training and there are firms that specialize in media training, as well. Some can provide emergency sessions on short notice. (To locate firms that provide these and other crisis communications services, visit the Society's website, www.stratsociety.org, click on Internet Yellow Pages, scroll down to the box called "public relations/communications" and select "crisis communications" from the drop-down box.)

However, it is not necessary to use an outside firm. Providing a few well-chosen pointers to the novice spokesperson, such as those listed above, can make a big difference in that individual's performance. Even if the spokesperson is experienced in speaking with the media, training around the specific messages you want to deliver is still critical to ensuring that your organization's position is effectively portrayed.

3.5. NEWS CONFERENCES

Determining Whether to Hold a News Conference

During a crisis, some interviews are conducted by telephone, others are conducted on site and still others take place during a news conference. News conferences can help you deliver information efficiently and effectively during a crisis—they eliminate the need to repeat the same information to many different individuals. However, there are times when it does *not* make sense to have a news conference. For example, you should not plan a news conference when issuing a prepared statement or conducting individual interviews would meet your objectives and satisfy media interest, when transportation is limited or erratic (as often occurs in the aftermath of a natural disaster) or when you do not have spokespersons who are prepared to answer questions. A news conference where a spokesperson simply reads a statement and refuses to answer questions is unnecessary and counterproductive.

Preparing for a News Conference

There is more to preparing for a news conference than just gearing up for the interview. There are also a host of logistical details that must be handled and press kits that must be prepared. The checklist in Figure 3-7 summarizes what you will need to do before a news conference begins.

Prepare written statements and question-and-answer documents for the news conference spokeperson(s) in advance. Add the prepared statement to the media kits that you should already have on hand for your other public relations activities. These media kits should include general "backgrounders" about the organization as well as maps and sometimes photographs.

Figure 3-7
News Conference Checklist

—— Coordinate timing with the crisis management team to ensure their availability.
—— Notify the press.
—— Invite other officials and physicians, as appropriate.
—— Notify hospital security.
—— Arrange for a photographer and/or videographer to document the event.
—— Reserve a room large enough to accommodate displays, reporters, TV cameras and lights.
—— Arrange for housekeeping services before the news conference, if needed, and afterwards.
—— Set up a podium with an organizational banner. Hang a backdrop, if needed.
—— Make the necessary arrangements for microphones, audio box and sound system.
—— Provide refreshments. *(Optional)*
—— Set up tables and chairs, taking care to accommodate photographers' sightlines.
—— Assemble any needed materials for display or distribution.
—— Brief your staff on the subject, spokesperson(s) and schedule.
—— Assign responsibility for all of the logistical arrangements on this list.

Conducting the Conference

We have all seen countless clips from news conferences on TV, but many public relations professionals have not had an opportunity to actually host a conference and run the show from start to finish. Here is the "play-by-play" of a typical news conference.

- Assign staffers to direct media to the briefing room.
- Assign a staffer to monitor and log the questions and answers closely.
- Log the names and affiliations of the media representatives who attend.
- Distribute press kits.
- Start your video and/or audio recorders.
- Open the conference. Identify yourself and introduce the team, including technical advisors.
- Describe the briefing format and schedule.
- Summarize information in the most recent news release and provide any updates.
- State whether injuries have occurred (when applicable).
- Describe the investigation and any corrective actions being performed (when applicable).
- Field questions from the audience.
- Announce the time of the next conference and thank the media for their participation and cooperation.

After the conference is over, debrief your staff, identify any problem areas with logistics or content and follow up as needed.

3.6. PREPARING WRITTEN STATEMENTS

The organization should make every effort to issue a public statement to the media within one hour of a news event. All public statements should use simple, specific language that supports the core messages and provides accurate, factual information. As you would in an interview, avoid jargon and speculation.

Most communications professionals have had ample opportunities to write news releases in the course of their everyday duties. The mechanics of the news release in crisis situations are no different. For those who are unfamiliar with writing news releases or who would like a refresher course, following are some tips for writing effective releases.

- **Put the most important information at the beginning**. The reader should know what the release is about from the first two paragraphs. This is where you provide the basics: who, what, when, where, why and how.

- **Avoid dramatic or unsubstantiated statements**. Crises are inherently dramatic. In some ways, it would be easier to write a feature article about the crisis than a press release. Remember, your purpose is not to create a compelling news story. That is a job for the media. Keep the release factual; avoid vivid descriptors and bold statements.

- **Keep your release to two pages or less**. If you cannot state your message in two pages, you are including too much detail or your message is unclear.

- **Include a contact**. The person whom reporters should contact for more information should be listed in the upper-right-hand corner of the press release or at the beginning or end of the document. This person should be familiar with all the news in the release and prepared to provide additional information.

- **Avoid jargon**. Reporters will not be as conversant with medical terminology as you are. Also, acronyms should always be spelled out.

- **Proofread**. First, spell-check on the computer. Then print the document out and proofread it. You will spot more errors this way than you will by reading it on the computer screen. If spelling and grammar are not your strengths, enlist the aid of a colleague.

Often, it will be necessary to release a statement acknowledging that something is going on before you know exactly what it is. This can be a difficult statement to write because there is little in the way of factual information to pull in. Following are some sample statements that can be used at this stage of the crisis.

At approximately _____ , we learned that _____ .
(time)   (brief description)

At this point, we cannot accurately report on the extent of the situation other than to say that it has involved _____ .
(brief description)

More information will be given to the media at _____ or as soon as it becomes available.
(time)

If you are asked additional questions before you are prepared to release more information, make a simple statement such as the following:

"That is all I can confirm at this time. We are very busy trying to deal with this situation and we'll need your patience for a short time. As soon as we have more information that has been confirmed, it will be disclosed to the public via the news media."

If casualties are involved, state that you will be unable to provide information about specific individuals until next-of-kin have been notified.

A communications strategy that centers around written statements, including press releases, letters and FAQs can be highly effective, especially in a crisis that is nonmedical in nature and expected to be of long duration.

3.7. EQUIPPING THE MEDIA CENTER

When the media assemble at your institution in large numbers to cover a crisis, it is a good idea to provide the reporters and their colleagues (photographers, videographers, producers, satellite technicians and others) with a central gathering place where you can hold briefings and they can set up their computers, microphones and cameras.

The number of media—and their composition—will determine the size of the room and how it will be provisioned. Keep in mind that a room that is adequate for most purposes may be too small in a crisis that attracts regional or national attention. (*See Case Study 3.2*, School Bus Accident, *and Case Study 3.3*, The CEO as Spokesperson in the Matthew Shepard Case, *for examples.*)

Here are some supplies and furnishings that will be useful in most media centers:

- Tables and chairs
- Plenty of electrical outlets
- Plenty of connections to the Internet (via phone or high-speed connection)
- Podium with microphone
- "Mult" box—a device allowing multiple sound recorders to be connected to a single podium microphone
- Fax machine (or machines) with dedicated lines
- Telephones and telephone directories (You may want to have the phones allow outgoing local, credit card or collect calls but not direct-dial long distance; they should be able to receive incoming calls.)
- Television receiver
- Press kits
- Miscellaneous office supplies (such as pens, pencils, felt-tip markers and scissors)
- Maps of the area
- Access to restrooms
- Food and beverages

In addition, if you have a staff member on hand at all times, establish a logbook to keep track of which media have used the center and any questions they might want answered.

CASE STUDY 3.1
WILDFIRES FORCE HOSPITAL EVACUATION

As the July 4 weekend approached in 1998, uncontrolled wildfires spread throughout Flagler County, Florida. Combined with red-flag fire conditions they created a risk of firestorms of such magnitude that federal and state emergency authorities decided to evacuate Flagler County's 40,000 residents, including the local hospital, Memorial Hospital-Flagler. It was the first time an entire county had been evacuated because of fire.

Memorial Hospital-Flagler is part of Memorial Health Systems, which was at that time a four-hospital, not-for-profit system in Volusia and Flagler Counties. The management team at Memorial Health Systems in Ormond Beach learned of the evacuation order at 10:30 a.m. on Friday, July 3, and immediately implemented its mutual aid plan. (Anticipating the possibility of an evacuation order, the hospitals already had been updating patient status records every four hours and creating discharge plans for all inpatients.)

All four of the Memorial Hospitals were dealing with medical emergencies resulting from the fire, but Memorial Hospital-Flagler was in the thick of the emergency action as the only hospital facility in Flagler County. Because the system's facility in DeLand, Memorial Hospital-West Volusia, was considered safe from the fires, Flagler's 32 inpatients would be transferred there. (The hospital also had agreements with other hospitals outside the system in case they were needed.) Five patients in a transitional care unit were sent to the system's flagship hospital in Ormond Beach, 20 miles south of Flagler's central wildfires.

A command center was established in the Memorial Health Systems boardroom in Ormond Beach; calls were already coming in from frightened evacuees and worried relatives. To assuage fears, the hospital worked with local broadcasters to make continual public service announcements about medical treatment availability, patient movements and the phone number relatives should call to confirm patients' whereabouts.

By midday, wheelchairs were ready at Memorial Hospital-Flagler—each accompanied by a nurse. The staff's first priority was to maintain calm—for patients *and* their families. But there was also the press to deal with—and they were desperate for a story.

Clare Watson, vice president, marketing and development, asked all patients whether they wanted to allow their photograph to be taken. None did. Mounting pressure and guerilla tactics on the part of the assembled "paparazzi" resulted in the Memorial staff members forming a human chain, shoulder to shoulder, around the wheelchairs to provide safe—and unseen—passage for the patients between the hospital and the waiting ambulances. In 45 minutes all patients and their nurse escorts were ready for the 25-mile trip to the West Volusia hospital—and safety.

Continued on page 72

CASE STUDY 3.1

CASE STUDY 3.1

WILDFIRES FORCE HOSPITAL EVACUATION *Continued from page 71*

Time was of the essence as the fire danger escalated with each passing minute. The procession drove at high speed over roads closed to other traffic, through firebreak lines, surrounded on both sides by smoldering white ash and the charred sticks of trees. Each ambulance was guided through the smoke by the taillights of the vehicle in front of it. It was difficult not to be apprehensive during this eerie voyage, but the nurses focused on keeping patients calm and comfortable. Twenty minutes later the procession had arrived at Memorial Hospital-West Volusia (now Florida Hospital Deland).

On the receiving end, each patient was personally greeted and escorted to a room by his or her assigned nurse. The West Volusia administrators had a master list of arriving patients that they checked against patients' wristbands, a huge benefit of having networked computer systems between the Memorial hospitals. A family waiting room had been set up to facilitate visits from concerned family members.

Meanwhile, back at Memorial Hospital-Flagler, a hardy skeleton staff remained on duty. The hospital served as a bunker for the FEMA (Federal Emergency Management Agency) firefighters. Sleeping facilities and meals were provided to the emergency crews by hospital administrators, nurses and staff.

Fortunately, the flames stayed just far enough away from the hospital to keep it from being endangered.

As the smoke cleared, and the hospitals returned to business as usual, stories of heroism and teamwork began to circulate among the staff. The stories varied: from the maintenance workers who gathered nurses' treasured wedding and baby albums from their threatened homes so that they could continue at their patients' bedsides to the engineers who carried oxygen tanks through the fires in their personal cars, ensuring a constant supply for threatened firefighters. The Memorial Health Systems marketing team gathered staff members' stirring memories on a video that was presented at a celebration dinner for the entire workforce a month after the emergency had passed.

LESSONS LEARNED

- Contingency plans should include relationships with other hospitals or long-term care facilities outside of your system and/or your geographic area. Memorial Hospital now plans to set up reciprocal emergency transfer agreements with hospitals on the west coast of Florida to use in the event of hurricanes or other emergencies.

- If your facility must be evacuated, coordination is the key. Memorial's evacuation went so smoothly because its staff started planning and coordinating with their sister hospital at the first hint that evacuation might be necessary.

- When large numbers of patients must be transferred to another facility for any reason, establish a central telephone number that relatives and other concerned parties can call to ascertain patients' whereabouts. Publicize this number through your hospital's website and through the media. Be sure the personnel who answer the telephone are informed so they can transfer calls appropriately.

- In an evacuation or similar emergency, the difference between providing the media with vital information and facilitating sensationalized reporting is crucial. Protect your patients from unwanted media attention by whatever means it takes, including the "human chain" that Memorial used to protect patients from photographers.

- Remember, your employees are in an emergency situation also. Employees will help each other if given half a chance. Encourage and facilitate acts of kindness among employees. Those whose work is not mission-critical in an emergency are often creative in finding ways to help those who must keep working.

- When the emergency is over, express your appreciation to employees in public as well as private, sincere and personal ways.

CASE STUDY 3.1

CASE STUDY 3.2
SCHOOL BUS ACCIDENT

In January 1999, Indian River Memorial Hospital in Vero Beach, FL, found itself at the center of a maelstrom following a school bus accident. A bus carrying grade school children collided with a citrus truck. The truck driver and one child on the bus were killed. Fourteen injured children were brought to Indian River Memorial Hospital, the largest hospital in the county.

Twenty minutes elapsed between the time the hospital received the call advising it of the accident and the arrival of the first victim. Even in that short time, the media had learned of the accident and TV stations were issuing news flashes about the accident—and interrupting the morning TV shows to do so.

The first challenge that director of marketing and public relations Michael Loyal faced was finding rooms for the media *and* parents that were close to the emergency department, but separated from each other so the parents' privacy could be maintained.

Several conference rooms near the department were transformed into waiting rooms/holding areas for families and staffed by hospital administrators. A separate room was designated for media. Naturally, reporters and photographers immediately wanted to interview—and photograph—the parents who were anxiously awaiting word about their children.

The hospital's staff were firm about protecting patient confidentiality in the hours immediately following the accident. The only information released to the media, in the beginning, focused on how many patients had been brought in and the nature and extent of their injuries. No names were released because not all parents had been notified yet.

Although none of the media resorted to extreme measures for gaining access to the emergency department, the hospital's layout became important at this stage. The hospital is located in a floodplain, so the emergency department is on the second floor.

Hospital security staff were posted to ensure that the ramp used by emergency vehicles was not blocked by media news vehicles. One reporter tried standing on the ramp and using a zoom lens to shoot pictures of the scene inside the emergency department. His efforts—and his line of sight—were blocked by hospital personnel.

Part of the reason for the media's overly zealous pursuit of the story lay in a misunderstanding of what it means to be a public hospital. As a public hospital owned by the hospital district, Indian River is subject to the Florida "sunshine" law, which requires that most hospital records and information be open to the public.

Some reporters believed that because Indian River is a public facility, they could have access to anything and anyone. The public relations staff quickly set the record straight: patients are entitled to the same protection and confidentiality rights at a public hospital as at a private one.

In addition to the on-site media, calls came in from distant outlets. The hospital's switchboard patched media calls through to public relations staff members' cell phones, and introduced each call so public relations staff instantly knew to whom they were speaking.

This technique meant that public relations staff did not need to check their voice mail, return to their offices, or try to listen for internal pages amid all the noise and confusion that accompanies a major trauma incident. (Staff cell phones are specially configured not to interfere with medical equipment, and thus can be used anywhere in the hospital.)

Loyal worked to get answers to the questions that everyone wanted to know: the names, ages and conditions of the victims being treated at Indian River—thereby simultaneously identifying children who were being treated at other hospitals. The hospital's patient registration staff, most of whom had been dispatched to the emergency department, provided the information to Loyal as soon as they received it. In addition to getting information from hospital staff, Loyal also sought to get a list of the children who had been on the bus from the School District.

It took an hour to develop a complete list of the young patients in the Indian River emergency department. For many of the waiting parents, it was the longest hour of their lives, despite the efforts by hospital administrators to alleviate their fears. Food service staff ensured that relatives (as well as news media elsewhere) were supplied with food and beverages. The hospital's efforts were hampered by the difficulty of distinguishing parents from other relatives, concerned friends or curious townsfolk who showed up in the emergency department.

Only two children were admitted for overnight observation; the others were treated and released. The school bus driver was critically injured and required immediate surgery. The media started asking about the bus driver immediately, but, in the absence of authorization from the patient or the patient's representative, the information released was limited to the standard "critical condition."

Because the driver's relatives were en-route from out-of-state, they could not approve any releases. The media questions soon turned to whether the driver had tested positive for drugs. The hospital declined to answer such questions, leaving those issues to the appropriate law enforcement agencies.

Loyal tracked all calls in a notebook he used as a media log and that greatly facilitated follow-up.

Continued on page 76

MEDIA RELATIONS IN A CRISIS

CASE STUDY 3.2

CASE STUDY 3.2

SCHOOL BUS ACCIDENT *Continued from page 75*

Continued from page 75

LESSONS LEARNED

- Indian River learned through this experience that its designated media room was too small. Now the hospital's boardroom is used as a media room. From time to time, review the appropriateness of rooms you have designated for special groups in times of crisis. How many people can the room hold comfortably? How does that number compare with the number who might *actually come on site* in a high-profile crisis? Choose a larger backup site to serve as your media room in case it is needed. Ask your telecommunications staff to install a bank of phone lines in the media room that can be activated in a crisis situation.

- Does the layout and/or design of your emergency department pose any security challenges in situations where you need to limit media access? If so, develop a contingency plan to deal with such challenges.

- Media, as well as the public at large, may not understand what it means to be a public hospital. Take every opportunity you can—especially *before* a crisis hits—to educate these critical audiences about the similarities and differences between public and private hospitals.

- Take full advantage of available communications technology. Cell phones that do not interfere with medical equipment and the ability to patch calls directly through to staff can be especially helpful in an emergency.

- Before an emergency happens, the public relations staff should be acquainted with the patient registration staff. In the chaos of an emergency department crowded with patients, relatives and the media, it is important for patient registration staff to know that it is "safe" for them to give patient information to public relations staff.

- Keep a log and record all media contacts—it helps to have a record of the reporters with whom you speak, when you spoke with them, their questions and your responses. During a crisis, jot this information down in longhand and transfer it to your computer later.

- No matter how good your crisis communications plan is, when a crisis hits, expect to find yourself filling roles to which you were not originally assigned. Be flexible.

- Avoid answering any media questions that relate to the culpability—legal or otherwise—of any parties involved in an incident. Such questions should be referred to the appropriate law enforcement agencies. Focus on information about the condition of patients during the time they are at your hospital—not on events that may or may not have happened to them before the patients arrived.

CHAPTER 3

CASE STUDY 3.3
THE CEO AS SPOKESPERSON IN THE MATTHEW SHEPARD CASE

The fatal attack on Matthew Shepard, a gay University of Wyoming student, drew interest and concern from people all over the world. On the evening of October 7, 1998, Matthew was admitted to Poudre Valley Hospital in Fort Collins, CO—the closest hospital with a neuro-intensive care unit—in critical condition with massive head trauma. He required a ventilator to breathe. Matthew had been pistol-whipped, tied to a fence and left in the cold to die.

On Matthew's arrival, the sheriff informed hospital public relations coordinator Gary Kimsey that he believed the beating was a hate crime. Gay rights had been featured in the news recently and this issue figured prominently in the upcoming national election. Kimsey knew immediately that this would be a big story. By October 9, calls had started coming in from all over the country and the world. The hospital decided to implement its crisis communications plan. In consultation with the hospital's other public relations coordinator, Armi Hall, Kimsey decided that, for a story of this magnitude, the hospital's CEO would be the best spokesperson.

Poudre Valley CEO Rulon Stacey had been at the hospital for about a year. He was an experienced executive, having previously served as CEO of another small hospital, but he had never dealt directly with the national media. The public relations staff believed that their young, personable CEO, who was good at thinking on his feet, would be a good spokesperson in this situation.

The public relations staff coached Stacey on the types of questions he would be asked and provided general guidelines for answering them. In the last analysis, however, preparation only goes so far. "There is no way to prepare anyone for an onslaught of the media" like the one that accompanied the attack on Matthew Shepard, Kimsey said. This being his first experience with programs such as *20/20* and *Hardcopy*, Stacey was "astounded" at how difficult the questions were, but his learning curve was steep. He quickly became adept at fielding all sorts of questions. He referred queries about what had happened before Matthew arrived at the hospital to law enforcement officials. He focused on Matthew's medical condition. And he conveyed genuine empathy for Matthew and his family. At the same time, he refused to be drawn into a discussion of issues that were beyond the hospital's purview.

There was one minor obstacle to implementing the crisis communications plan. The area designated as the media room was located on the fourth floor of the hospital, steps away from Matthew's bedside in the neuro-intensive care unit. Matthew's parents were intent on protecting his privacy, with pictures strictly prohibited. So the media set up camp outside in front of the hospital.

The hospital public relations staff kept a steady stream of food, doughnuts and coffee going to reporters in the parking lot. There was a steady stream of information as well, with news con-

Continued on page 78

CASE STUDY 3.3 *Continued from page 77*
THE CEO AS SPOKESPERSON IN THE MATTHEW SHEPARD CASE

ferences held every six hours around the clock. This meant that Stacey and the public relations staffers were there nonstop, going home only to shower and change clothes.

Matthew's parents, who had been in the Middle East, could not get there until the evening of October 9. During the long days while Matthew lay unconscious, the hospital did everything it could to satisfy the media's need for information and the public's desire to express their sympathy, concern and outrage to Matthew's parents. Medical updates were posted on the hospital's website, generating more than 450,000 hits (and nearly shutting down the site). The hospital also created an e-mail address on its site for well-wishers to send electronic get-well messages, which logged nearly 2,000 e-mails. Hall and Kimsey scrambled to answer more than 1,000 phone calls, many from the public. They quickly set up a phone-in line with a recorded message to redirect the nonmedia calls. They also worked with Matthew's parents to write a statement for media release, thanking the public for their good wishes and telling the poignant story of Matthew's life. At the parents' request, Stacey read the statement at a news conference. Finally, the hospital helped get out the word about the fund that had been established for people to make donations in lieu of sending flowers. The last news conference was held at 4:30 a.m. on October 12 to announce Matthew's death.

This was a crisis that had a definite ending, at least from the hospital's perspective. After Matthew died, the media moved on to Laramie, WY, where Matthew's alleged attackers were in custody. Aaron James McKinney was later convicted of felony murder and sentenced to two consecutive life sentences without possibility of parole. Matthew's parents intervened to spare him the death penalty.

LESSONS LEARNED

- A story that draws national or international interest may well benefit from having the CEO serve as spokesperson. The CEO's presence can lend credibility and point up the organization's understanding of the importance of the story.

- Before the interview or news conference, review principles of crisis communications/media relations with your CEO. (*See Section 4.7 for more information.*)

- Never assume that the room you have designated for the media will actually accommodate them if the story becomes national or international in scope. Most of the time that is not likely to happen; nevertheless, have a much bigger space in mind—think in terms of *hundreds* of reporters instead of a few or a few dozen.

INTERNAL COMMUNICATIONS IN A CRISIS

4.1. OVERVIEW

Have you developed internal communications that are perceived as credible, timely and accurate? If so, you have gone a long way toward ensuring effective internal communications during a crisis because your audience will be predisposed to trust you and believe what you are telling them.

Effective internal crisis communication is essential to avoid confusion and distractions, maintain productivity, provide effective customer service and support rapid resolution of the crisis. During a crisis, remember that you are modeling to employees the communication styles and the messages that they will be using to communicate with patients, the public and each other. The communicator's approach to internal communications during a crisis should include the following steps:

- **Reassure your audience that the crisis is under control—at least in terms of the organization's role**. This is a key step. If employees are not confident that the organization is equipped to handle the crisis, problems will multiply exponentially and all subsequent communication efforts will be compromised.

- **Make sure everyone understands the situation and knows the facts**. As always, be concise; avoid rambling and speculation. Your messages should be empathetic but at the same time, they should focus on the facts and on what can be controlled. Dispelling rumors and misinformation is a part of this process. Create an atmosphere where employees are comfortable asking about rumors—this is one of the most effective ways of stopping the rumor mill.

- **Build in opportunities to address concerns**. Question-and-answer sessions should be an integral component of every internal communications update. This process builds trust between staff and the leadership team.

- **Check periodically for understanding**. Be sensitive to any potential cultural differences that may affect employees' interpretations of and reactions to the crisis.

- **Provide regular and timely updates**. When an organization functions in crisis mode for an extended period, the initial shock subsides, employees adjust, and there may be little in the way of real "news." Updates may become less frequent but they should not stop altogether. After the initial adrenaline rush fades, reality sets in and depression and fatigue often go along with it. At this stage, people need to realize that the crisis will not continue indefinitely. They also need the ongoing support and camaraderie that their colleagues can provide.

The first communication during a crisis sets the tone of subsequent events and sets the stage for all that follows. This crucial first message to staff should do the following:

- **Briefly summarize what has occurred**. Use clear, concise language and avoid medical jargon. Do not minimize—or dramatize—the situation. Present the facts. If there is information that is not yet known, mention that fact but do not speculate.

- **Explain what caused the crisis** if the causes are simple, straightforward and unambiguous. This is usually the case in a natural disaster. However, in other crises, the cause may be in question so do not dwell on it—but do not avoid it either.

- **Indicate what is being done currently and how long the crisis is expected to last**. Concrete action steps foster a sense of control and help staff focus on what is actually happening rather than worrying about what *might* happen.

- **Acknowledge the emotions that people may be experiencing**. Reactions will vary. It is important for everyone to feel safe to express emotions. You can help staff control their own reactions and keep a sense of proportion through your own communications style. Show that you care; avoid a detached or impassive demeanor. But don't "lose it"—people want clarity, strength and confidence from their leaders.

- **Identify the individuals who are in charge**. If different people are handling different aspects of the crisis, make sure that responsibilities are clear.

- **Reinforce your commitment to keeping everyone informed**. Employees should be confident that you will continue to keep them "in the loop."

- **Describe the communications channels that will be used for crisis updates**. Will you be using voice mail, e-mail, the intranet or other channels? Will meetings be held?

- **Explain any interim operating procedures thoroughly**. Provide this information in writing as well as posting it on the intranet, when appropriate, and/or on nursing unit and other departmental bulletin boards.

Subsequent updates should include the following:

- A brief recap of the crisis
- Progress and new information since the last communication
- Any corrections or changes to previous information
- Clarification as needed, based on audience feedback
- Emotional support and validation

Incorporate feedback channels into your crisis communications techniques. Use paper forms, hotlines and e-mail questionnaires to check understanding and monitor the morale of different audiences. Sometimes employees are hesitant to speak up in a group setting. Also, concerns may develop or questions may arise between briefings. Using a variety of communications channels mitigates these problems (Alcorn 2001).

4.2. Crisis-Specific Considerations

Dealing with the media in a crisis is complex in many ways, but in at least one respect it is simple—the media's goals are always the same, no matter what kind of crisis is occurring—they want to get the best story and get it out as quickly as possible. Things are not so straightforward with internal audiences, however. Different kinds of crises lead to different kinds of communications challenges. In a disaster that involves multiple casualties, healthcare professionals may be torn between their strong sense of responsibility to help the victims and their intense concern about their own families and homes, possibly about their own safety. Situations that involve allegations against a fellow employee or the organization as a whole may result in a different range of conflicting emotions that can interfere with employees' ability to work and exacerbate the crisis overall. The following sections provide guidelines to help you communicate effectively with internal audiences in different kinds of crises.

4.3. When an Employee Is Accused of Wrongdoing

When a hospital employee is accused of wrongdoing in connection with his or her job—especially if the allegations involve patients—fellow employees often react with shock, disbelief and fear. They may experience denial—refusing to believe that their colleague could have done anything wrong and even lashing out against the media who report on the event and the public relations staff who work with the media. On the other hand, a few employees may claim they suspected the individual was up to no good. Some may even feel guilty because they believe they could have averted the problem.

In circumstances like these, ignoring the issue only feeds the rumor mill, distracts employees from their work and lowers morale. It is better to acknowledge the issue, ideally before the media do. An all-staff memo or e-mail will suffice in many situations, but in a high-profile case that is expected to garner a lot of media attention, all-staff meetings on every shift may be preferable.

- **Know what information may be released.** Arrests are a matter of public record, so it is OK to disclose the name of an employee who has been arrested. But you have an obligation to protect the privacy of an employee who is under investigation, either internally or by law enforcement agencies, if an arrest has not been made.

- When appropriate, **disclose that the employee has been removed from his job** and will not be reinstated unless and until hospital management is satisfied that no wrongdoing has occurred. Specify whether the employee was suspended or terminated.

- **Do not speculate about the employee's guilt, innocence or possible motivations.** This means that you should neither express confidence in the employee's innocence nor condemn his alleged actions, regardless of what your personal opinions and beliefs are about the situation. Emphasize that the investigation will be thorough and fair.

- A CEO or other executive acting as spokesperson on this issue should **reassure employees** that this is believed to be an isolated incident that in no way reflects on other employees. The leader should affirm confidence and pride in employees as a group.

- **Explain how to handle inquiries from patients and community members**. Model suggested language for employees rather than just summarizing the desired approach. Emphasize that media inquiries should be directed to public relations.

- When appropriate, **reassure employees that policies and procedures are being reviewed** to ensure that similar incidents will not recur.

Case Study 4.1, *Theft of Patient Identity Information*, describes an incident in which a temporary employee stole patient identity information. The hospital launched a full-disclosure communications campaign that included internal question-and-answer documents as well as letters to patients and statements to the media. This proactive approach minimized the negative effects of the incident.

Case Study 4.2, *Unexplained Medical Findings*, tells the story of a hospital's investigation of events surrounding unauthorized administration of insulin injections to a number of nondiabetic patients.

4.4. When an Organization Is Accused of Wrongdoing

Many organizations avoid internal communications during a "crisis of confidence" because they do not know what to say or how to say it. This is a mistake. Even during the worst of times, communicating will help people remain calm and productive. Pretending that everything is business-as-usual or being secretive only makes a difficult situation worse.

On an organizationwide scale, allegations of wrongdoing can involve a risk of loss of accreditation or certification, which—in the worst-case scenario—could result in suspension or termination of certain clinical services or even overall operations. Employees may be shaken by the idea that their hospital could have knowingly done something wrong. Some may be apprehensive about what this will mean for their job security.

- **Do not make false reassurances**. The nature of these situations is such that it is often difficult to know all the facts early on. Emphasize that the hospital is taking all appropriate steps to investigate the situation, make any necessary changes or corrections and avoid negative sanctions.

- **Focus on the big picture**. Continue to link your communication messages to your goals and strategic priorities. "Living" your organizational values provides security and reassurance to your internal constituencies. Demonstrate that you are continually monitoring external influences for their impact on your business strategy.

- Once again, **explain how to handle inquiries from patients and community members**. Model suggested language for employees rather than just summarizing the desired approach. Provide talking points, when appropriate. Emphasize that media inquiries should be directed to public relations.

- **Monitor the impact on your staff**. Track key personnel metrics such as absenteeism, retention levels and productivity. When business has been significantly affected, conduct regular pulse surveys and focus groups to assess changes in people's attitudes, trust in leadership and morale.

- **Use informal opportunities to assess morale as well**. Be visible—leadership visibility is critical to restoring and maintaining employees' trust in the organization. Listen and respond to employees who want to express their concerns.

4.5. WHEN DISASTER STRIKES

In a natural disaster such as a hurricane or a manmade disaster such as a terrorist attack, employees are likely to be affected along with everyone else. Employees may be busier than they have ever been, caring for victims of the disaster while they cope with worries about their relatives, their homes and their futures. All the while, they may feel they have no one to whom they can turn for help because all hospital resources are consumed by caring for community members.

Public relations staff must "care for the caregivers" during a crisis by providing them the information they need for their own peace of mind and wellbeing. Too often, during a crisis employees rely on their coworkers for information. Using these informal communications channels, many employees receive vital information late, if at all. Depending on the nature and scope of the disaster, important internal communications information during a disaster can include the following:

- **Information about employee safety**. Have areas of the hospital been shut down to prevent damage from a storm or other natural disaster, or because of such damage? Is the rest of the structure expected to be safe? If not, where should employees in affected areas go? In the event of a biochemical or nuclear incident, what are the risks to employees? What is the hospital doing to ensure their safety?

- **Transportation arrangements** for employees who have difficulty getting to or from the hospital because of the disaster. This may include carpools, volunteers with four-wheel-drive vehicles or police or fire department transport.

- **Finding out about schedules and schedule changes** during the disaster recovery period. Employees calling in to find out when they should report for work or to report that they are unable to report can quickly overload the telephone system in a disaster.

- **Provisions for emergency loans, cash advances and/or temporary housing** for employees whose homes are temporarily or permanently uninhabitable as a result of the disaster. This may include "camping out" and/or taking showers at the hospital and help with finding kennel care for pets.

- **Special arrangements for meals** and cafeteria discounts that may be in effect during the disaster recovery period.

- Arrangements for hospital-sponsored **child care** for employees who are working additional or different shifts. Employees' regular child-care arrangements may be disrupted by the disaster.

- **Changes in holiday, vacation or sick leave policies** that will be in effect during the disaster recovery period. For example, in the wake of Hurricane Andrew, Baptist Health South Florida allowed employees who needed extra money to cash in holiday and vacation time. They also developed a leave-sharing plan to allow coworkers to help each other. (*See Case Study 4.3.*) During a prolonged ice storm, Canton-Potsdam Hospital authorized some employees to go into the community to help out, and counted the work as though they were at the hospital. (*See Case Study 1.2.*)

- **Emotional and psychosocial support services for employees**, including individual counseling, group sessions, prayer or memorial services and employee assistance programs.

- **Changes in patient care procedures**. Hospitals are complex organizations. When procedures that involve patient care are changed abruptly, the risk of errors increases. Procedures in a host of areas—such as clinical credentialing, processing medical records and dispensing medications—may be different in a disaster involving multiple casualties. If the hospital has a comprehensive crisis plan, it will outline most, if not all of these contingencies. Clinical managers—not public relations managers—will be responsible for disseminating this information to patient care staff. Most clinical managers are not communications professionals so they may appreciate your advice and suggestions for making this information easier to understand and ensuring that it reaches the intended audiences.

Although it is not public relations' responsibility to develop or implement employee support services, communicating them to employees is an important role for public relations staff. The more support the caregivers have, the better equipped they will be to care for disaster victims. Before a crisis comes, work with your management team to find out what contingency plans have been established. This will facilitate communications later on.

Case Study 4.3, *"Andrew Zero, Baptist Won,"* shows how a hospital came through for its employees—as well as its community—in the aftermath of a major hurricane.

4.6. WHEN EMPLOYEES GO OUT ON STRIKE

One of the most difficult internal communications challenges occurs when employees strike. The most important thing to know about communicating with employees during a strike is that your legal counsel should guide your communications every step of the way—both the channels and the content. In many cases, the hospital's human resources executive is familiar with the various legal requirements that apply in this situation and can provide appropriate guidance as well. Significant sanctions can result when communicators make missteps that have legal ramifications.

Case Study 4.4, *Strike*, describes the communications challenges that one hospital dealt with successfully during a strike that affected every department in the hospital.

AVOIDING TELEPHONE SYSTEM OVERLOAD DURING A DISASTER

In a disaster of regional scope, whether natural or manmade, peoples' first thoughts will be about the safety of their loved ones. On September 11, hospital telephone systems in the New York City area were almost immediately overwhelmed with calls by staff calling out to inquire about their families. In two hospitals, the system crashed for several hours. The system was overwhelmed in the first few minutes by normal and predictable reactions from staff. Then came a second wave—this time of incoming telephone calls. Off-duty staff members started calling in to find out how they could help. Many emergency management plans did not have a provision for staff members to communicate with the hospital.

Recommendations:

- Work with the staff. Find ways to deal with staff concerns while managing their actions. Have it written into the plan that staff are to restrict outgoing calls to specific phones, and for a specified period of time.

- Establish in advance that one of the responsibilities of off-duty staff during an emergency is to meet at a certain location. They should not call individual supervisors or go directly to their department. This scatters resources, delays deployment and causes unnecessary confusion.

Source: 2001. *Aftermath: Lessons learned about emergency preparedness from the September 11 crisis.* MedSafe, Inc., www.medsafe.com. October.

4.7. HELPING THE CEO COMMUNICATE WITH EMPLOYEES DURING A CRISIS

According to Davis & Company, an employee communications consulting firm based in Glen Rock, NJ, the very skills that propel senior leaders up the corporate ladder—sharp analysis of situations, the ability to make decisions, act quickly and never waver or look back—work against them when it comes to communicating with employees during a crisis. When appropriate, coach your CEO on the following basic communications principles:

- Tell the truth. Employees have more respect for someone who tells them the good, the bad and the ugly, rather than someone who tries to gloss over the negative points.

- Have a clearly defined communications role. Leaders need to be role models for the rest of the company. If they communicate, other managers and employees will follow suit. Great communicators mingle with employees. The more leaders talk with employees, the more natural it becomes.

- Streamline messages into bite-sized chunks. Employees need time to absorb and reflect on information in order to learn.

- Leverage the power of storytelling. Personal accounts and anecdotes stay with employees more than abstract ideas do. Avoid clichés and slogans. Employees can spot "corporate speak" at 100 paces.

- Repeat, repeat, repeat. Often, leaders are so immersed in a crisis that they could recite the key points in their sleep. But employees need to hear the message many times before it really sinks in.

- Communicate the "why" first. The "why" is just as important as the what and the how, yet it is often lost in the shuffle. Operations-oriented CEOs may be focusing on fixing the problem. They need to understand that they will get more support from employees if they explain it first. Telling employees why something is being done helps them put a message into context.

- Don't wait until all the facts are in. Employees would prefer to find out what is known sooner and get more information later, rather than not being told anything until every last detail is in place (Davis & Company 2002).

The investment of time and effort made in internal communications during a crisis will be returned in the form of better crisis outcomes in the short term as well as by enhanced employee satisfaction and retention after the crisis is over.

CASE STUDY 4.1
THEFT OF PATIENT IDENTITY INFORMATION

In preparation for compliance with HIPAA, many hospitals are focusing on protecting patients' confidential medical information. But the nonmedical information that every hospital maintains on its patients also presents security risks, as Boston's renowned Dana-Farber Cancer Institute learned in the summer of 2000.

Dana-Farber discovered that a temporary worker hired to update nonmedical information had apparently stolen patient identity information, including names, addresses and Social Security numbers. This was not a case of sophisticated cybertheft—the woman simply took a computer printout. She was observed in the act by a coworker, who duly reported it to security.

Dana-Farber immediately contacted a police detective in the city's fraud unit and the police launched an investigation. At the same time, Steve Singer, then chief of communications for Dana-Farber, joined an ad hoc crisis team. The team was chaired by the chief operating officer and consisted of representatives from communications, security, patient relations, human resources, quality improvement, risk management and access management, the department where the temporary employee had worked, as well as the hospital's in-house legal counsel. Members of Dana-Farber's Patient and Family Advisory Council were also asked for their concerns and input.

Within two days of learning about the incident, Dana-Farber had outlined a strategy that reflected its commitment to take a proactive, patients-first approach. Patients affected by the theft would be held harmless and the hospital would cover any losses. Management wanted to take all precautions in order to protect their patients. At first, the hospital had no way of knowing how many patients would be at risk of identity theft and fraud. Ultimately, it turned out that only three people were affected, but it could have been much more extensive.

The hospital also took steps to prevent a recurrence.

- Plans to perform criminal background checks on all prospective employees were fast-tracked and expanded to include temporary workers.
- All temporary employee arrangements were consolidated through a single agency that provides background checks.
- Online medical records were redesigned to minimize utilization and printing of Social Security numbers. Employees with access to Social Security numbers were given a higher level of security clearance and made individually identifiable through an audit trail.

Continued on page 88

CASE STUDY 4.1
THEFT OF PATIENT IDENTITY INFORMATION *Continued from page 87*

THE COMMUNICATIONS CAMPAIGN

The immediate challenge was to develop a comprehensive communications campaign for internal and external audiences.

- Letters were sent to all 12,000 patients who had been seen at the hospital during the four months that the worker was there, including the families of deceased patients. A translated version was sent to Spanish-speaking patients. The letter explained what had happened, provided information about how to contact credit agencies to request a credit check and a credit block, gave a toll-free hotline number for help and offered to reimburse patients for any expenses associated with obtaining the credit report.

- That same toll-free Patient Assistance Line was established at the hospital for concerned patients or family members to talk with patient relations staff who could answer questions and refer patients to an attorney retained by the hospital. The attorney had financial expertise and experience with credit bureaus that would enable him to help anyone who experienced any problems stemming from this incident. (About 100 of the 12,000 people who received notifications called the hotline.)

- Talking points in a frequently-asked-questions format were distributed internally via e-mail to staff with patient contact and to senior Institute officials. The talking points clarified exactly what had happened, how Dana-Farber found out about it, how many patients were potentially affected, what staff could do to help patients with questions, what steps individuals should take to check their credit and what the hospital was doing to prevent a recurrence.

- Letters were sent to the Board of Trustees.

- An article was written for Dana-Farber's internal newsletter, which is available to all patients, families and staff.

The hospital had also planned to issue a written statement to the media but unrelated events soon changed this plan and compelled Dana-Farber to adopt a more high-profile media strategy.

TIMING IS EVERYTHING

Dana-Farber knew that the matter would go public as soon as the patient letters went out and it was prepared for that. But, as fate would have it, the perpetrator in the Dana-Farber case was arraigned on the same day and in the same courthouse as an alleged gunman in a highly publicized crime. The entire local press corps was on hand to cover the arraignment of the shooter and were in place to observe the proceedings in the Dana-Farber case.

Dana-Farber would have liked the luxury of having a few more days before going public with the news—it was not quite ready to send out the 12,000 letters. With the sudden surge in media interest, the hospital realized that its plans for issuing a brief written statement were no longer adequate; the hospital would have to move proactively and emphasize that it was fully engaged and serious about resolving this problem.

With that in mind, Dana-Farber conducted individual interviews in person and by phone with five local TV stations, the two major daily newspapers and the Associated Press. Its main messages focused on explaining what had happened, assuring the patients and the public that no medical information was involved and reinforcing the idea that the hospital would do everything in its power to ensure that patients would be held harmless and that medical care would not be affected.

The public seemed to recognize and appreciate that Dana-Farber had made a genuine commitment to its patients. Media attention lasted for only a couple of days. The hospital's prompt action in taking ownership of the problem, communicating clearly and openly and ensuring that everything possible was done to mitigate the situation averted a potential media crisis.

A *postscript:* After reviewing Joint Commission materials on sentinel events and discussing the matter with the state department of public health, the hospital determined that this incident did not constitute a sentinel event. However, after seeing news reports, the Joint Commission contacted the hospital asking for information about the incident and the hospital's response to it. In its reply to the Joint Commission, the hospital summarized the incident and the actions that were being taken to prevent a recurrence. It also emphasized the open communications around the incident with patients, staff and other audiences. The Joint Commission took no further action.

LESSONS LEARNED

- Get your story out the first day so it does not look like you are being pushed by events. Be as open as possible. Provide as much information as you can as soon as possible so that the story is not prolonged by information coming out in bits and pieces over a longer period of time. Do as much work as you can before the story goes public and move quickly when it does. Do not base your plans on the assumption that a story can be kept confidential.

- When appropriate, frame the story in the context of a larger national problem. For example, identity theft is a growing concern nationwide; a hospital involved with this issue could take the opportunity to educate consumers about how they can protect themselves.

- Keep your management group inclusive, and stay focused on what is best for patients and their families.

CASE STUDY 4.2
UNEXPLAINED MEDICAL FINDINGS

Few situations are as difficult for hospital communicators to deal with as those that involve a cloud of suspicion over a nurse or other employee with patient contact.

That was the situation encountered by a hospital (which chooses to remain anonymous) in the summer of 1998.

Routine blood work revealed that four patients–all over age 90 and all having been treated on one nursing unit—had experienced episodes of unexplained low blood sugar over the course of a 30-day period.

The hospital's risk management, quality assurance and security protocols were implemented, and a preliminary internal investigation revealed that the patients had most likely received insulin injections even though no physician had ordered it.

When a drug is administered with no order on file, hospitals are required to report the incident to the appropriate state agency, which in turn reports it to the Centers for Medicare & Medicaid Services. Furthermore, it qualifies as a Joint Commission "sentinel event." Hospitals also must report such incidents to local police departments.

The hospital in this study duly made its reports, and the three agencies involved each launched independent investigations, even as the hospital continued its own.

None of the patients died or were directly harmed as a result of the insulin administration, but some later died of unrelated causes, thus further compounding the difficulty of the investigation.

As soon as the incidents were reported to state and federal authorities, they became public information. Local newspapers picked up the story and began making inquiries. Their first inquiries were directly to several individuals in hospital administration, who each made statements that showed up in the paper the next day. The large headlines gave the story a tabloid feel: "Unexplained blood sugar drops at local hospital; state agencies involved." The story was rapidly picked up by other media.

In this case, the hospital's situation was compounded by the fact that the public relations function had only been in existence for six months. Responsibility for the newly created public relations function was assigned to the director of marketing. The director had to act swiftly.

After reviewing the situation with the CEO, the director contacted the state hospital association vice president of public relations and briefed him on the situation. The director then sought advice and a referral to a public relations agency well-versed in such situations.

The key message points developed by the hospital and the agency were as follows:

- The events had been discovered through the hospital's internal security and quality control processes.
- The hospital followed all protocols and reported the event to the appropriate agencies.
- Patient confidentiality prevented the hospital from commenting on the specifics.
- The hospital's top priority was—and remained—ensuring the safety and security of its patients.

Despite the combined efforts of the hospital and the agency, a week after the story broke, someone inside the hospital spoke to the media anonymously and reported that a nurse was under suspicion.

The investigations had necessitated site visits by regulatory and accreditation authorities. Interest in the story spiked again as the media found a new angle: reporting that the hospital was in danger of losing its Medicare certification. The hospital countered with another message: it expected to come through the site inspections with flying colors.

At the conclusion of the site visits, one newspaper printed the inspectors' recommendations. The hospital acknowledged that the printed recommendations were accurate and added no other comments.

The hospital's strategy in this ordeal was not to engage in a dialogue with the media, but rather to use the media as a conduit for its message, essentially speaking through the media to its various publics.

After approximately three months, media interest trailed off when no conclusive findings emerged from the investigations. No determination of criminal activity was ever made.

Because the hospital noted a decrease in volume over the next few months, they retained a marketing research firm to conduct focus groups in the community. The results were reassuring: the change in operating indicators was apparently unrelated to the incident in question; damage to the hospital's image and reputation from the incident was somewhere between negligible and nonexistent.

Continued on page 92

CASE STUDY 4.2

CASE STUDY 4.2

UNEXPLAINED MEDICAL FINDINGS *Continued from page 91*

LESSONS LEARNED

- Most hospitals have never experienced allegations of wrongdoing by an employee, but it can happen anywhere. Have crisis communications policy/procedures in place before it does.

- After the incident, the hospital developed a corporate media relations strategy. Media relationship management—with local reporters, editors and opinion leaders—is key to optimizing the outcome of any crisis. Media relationships must be in place and ongoing before the crisis hits.

- An internal crisis demonstrates to top management the value of the public relations, media relations and marketing functions. In the aftermath, reinforce to executives and board members that, in any future crisis, public relations staff need to be brought on board and allowed to take control of the situation as early as possible.

- Understand that the first statements made to the media by the organization set the tone for media relations and message control for the duration of the crisis.

- At the first sign of a problem involving hospital employees or physicians, the management team should refine its strategy and determine appropriate responses.

- Notify all staff to direct calls of inquiry to the hospital public relations director for triage and referral.

- Draw on resources such as state hospital associations for suggestions and referrals. It is also advisable to keep them apprised in case they receive media calls about the incident.

- The value of having outside counsel/agencies confirm "what your gut is telling you" should not be underestimated. When the stakes are high, the return is well worth the investment.

- Formally review what went right and what went wrong with crisis procedures. Learn from experience and apply it.

CASE STUDY 4.3
"ANDREW ZERO, BAPTIST WON"

That was the headline Baptist Health South Florida's employee communications department printed on the System's newsletter, *Vocal Chord,* in October 1992. The entire issue was dedicated to coverage of Hurricane Andrew's impact on the System.

PROLOGUE

Baptist vice president Lee Huntley (who is now CEO of Baptist Hospital of Miami) was on call on Saturday, August 22, 1992, when a local TV station reported that Hurricane Andrew was expected to make a direct hit on Miami early Monday. Huntley asked all available department heads and managers to come to an early Sunday emergency hurricane preparedness meeting.

Staffing schedules—two teams: one team to work, one to sleep—were set up to ensure that the storm would not keep employees on the next shift from coming to work. Employees were permitted to bring their children with them if they had concerns about their safety.

On Sunday, "Everyone made their phone calls, then went home to prepare their homes as best they could. The scenario was, you said goodbye to your family, then came back to work. It was a very hard thing to do," recalled Huntley.

While the hospital was boarding up windows, moving supplies and preparing thousands of sandwiches, the marketing and public relations staff hand-delivered the first of what would turn out to be many hurricane bulletins to employees. They also contacted the media to inform them that all elective surgeries were being cancelled until further notice.

As Sunday night wore on, employees slept on office floors, on lounge chairs—wherever they could. At 1 a.m., a tile blew through the window of the office where the public relations staff had taken refuge. "That's when we knew it was a real storm," said Anne Streeter, assistant vice president of marketing and public relations. "There was no more sleep that night."

In the predawn darkness, the engineering staff braved "horizontal" rain and flying debris to make a repair that was threatening the hospital's vital backup generators. Meanwhile, the nursing staff were busy moving patients out of their rooms and into the hallways, away from breaking windows. While patients escaped harm, some computers that were positioned near windows did not. Damage to Baptist facilities was significant, but it paled in comparison with the devastation in the surrounding communities.

Continued on page 94

CASE STUDY 4.3
"ANDREW ZERO, BAPTIST WON" *Continued from page 93*

AFTERMATH

By 9:30 a.m. on Monday, the hospital's emergency room was "wall-to-wall people." The computers were inoperable; there was no water or air conditioning and—typical of South Florida in August—it was a sweltering day.

Employees—in what was dubbed the "toilet brigade"—filled trashcans with water from the hydrotherapy pool and poured them down the toilets to make them "flush." This was a full-time job in itself. Everyone worked overtime in brutally hot conditions—one operating room technician even passed out during a C-section. Patients in the cardiac care unit who could not tolerate the heat were transferred to other facilities.

In a scene reminiscent of *M.A.S.H.,* shell-shocked patients streamed into the emergency room with lacerations, broken bones and other wounds, even heart attacks brought on by stress.

The Baptist staff quickly dispensed with traditional hierarchical attention to titles and position. *Everyone* pitched in to help—a cadre of nurses from all parts of the hospital worked side-by-side with administrators, physicians, secretaries, volunteers and even relatives of employees in the ER. For some, their shift lasted 36 hours straight.

The Hurricane Command Post was staffed by hospital vice presidents and served as the central information point throughout the crisis.

Also on Monday morning, local TV crews converged on the hospital. "There were two or three TV crews here at once, plus newspapers and radio stations from around the country calling constantly," said Adrienne Sylver, public relations manager. "At the same time you were on the phone with a reporter from Indianapolis who wanted to know how many babies delivered the night of the hurricane were named Andrew, you had CNN on the other line asking how many patients we had in the ER. As soon as you hung up, local TV stations showed up in the ER."

When they weren't handling media calls (or parking cars for patients, making sandwiches or distributing donated clothing), the public relations staff photocopied 19,000 hurricane updates and hand-delivered them—in the beginning, twice daily, then tapering down over the next two weeks.

The public relations staff also helped track down doctors and relayed messages between doctors and patients. None of the phones in the hospital worked properly—including cell phones and beepers.

CARING FOR THE CAREGIVERS

When a crisis of this magnitude strikes, employees will be affected along with everyone else in the community. As soon as the storm hit Miami, phone lines went down and employees were unable to call their families.

Arlenna Williams, assistant vice president, recalled, "So many of Baptist's staff lost everything. The people who were killing themselves at the hospital couldn't communicate with their own families— we couldn't provide false hopes; all we could do was listen as people vented their feelings.

"You express concern and sympathy and you deal with the moment. One nurse took one look at me in the hallway and just started to cry. Her husband and children were in another town and she said, 'I don't know if they're alive.' I asked one of the National Guard [troops] to check it out. It was a miracle that he even found her home, but her family was OK."

Fully half of Baptist's employees sustained severe damage to or total loss of their homes. The hospital appealed to the community for help finding housing for employees, and the employees' relatives and friends throughout the country launched food and clothing drives.

Public relations' hurricane updates featured news about the many support services that had been put in place for employees. Each is worthy of consideration as you develop crisis communications plans:

- Arrangements were made for employees to get a $100 cash advance on their paychecks three days after the storm.
- The cafeteria increased employee discounts to 50 percent and accepted payroll deductions from employees who were low on cash.
- The hospital's day-care center was made available 24 hours a day for employees' children, regardless of whether they were normally registered there.
- Disaster relief funds were made available through the hospital's retirement fund, and through the Sunshine Fund, an account that already existed to help employees in times of disaster or financial need.
- Employees were given the ability to cash in holiday/vacation and sick time and an opportunity to borrow future holiday/vacation time. Later, a leave-sharing plan was developed to allow coworkers to help each other.
- The Credit Union offered special low-interest loans.
- A corps of volunteers recruited by the pastoral care and construction management departments helped repair employees' homes.
- Roofing materials were purchased by the hospital and made available to employees at contractors' cost.
- Numerous speakers, including insurance adjusters, contractors and FEMA (Federal Emergency Management Agency) representatives, gave presentations at the hospital.
- More than 1,100 employees learned coping strategies at employee "help sessions."
- The medical library coordinated a carpooling effort so employees who had relocated or whose vehicles were damaged could come to work.

Continued on page 96

CASE STUDY 4.3

CASE STUDY 4.3

"*ANDREW ZERO, BAPTIST WON*" *Continued from page 95*

Departments from throughout the hospital contributed to the communications effort in many ways, but it still was the responsibility of public relations to gather the information and disseminate it to employees. At the same time, public relations had to deal with a deluge of national media attention. The public relations staff recruited its own volunteers: professional colleagues from other area organizations who willingly came in and helped.

LESSONS LEARNED

- In a natural disaster, employees will be affected. Know what the hospital's plans are for meeting employees' immediate needs for food, clothing, shelter, childcare and cash.

- Develop and keep current information about support services that will be available for employees, including counseling and assistance in dealing with rebuilding.

- Be prepared to disseminate information the "old-fashioned" way because e-mail is likely to be down. Even if e-mail is operational, it may not reach everyone. People are often not at their regular workstations during a crisis of this nature—they are apt to be found serving meals in the cafeteria or helping on the front lines.

- Fallen trees, flooding and debris can make roads all but impassable for most vehicles in the aftermath of a hurricane. This makes it difficult for employees and physicians to reach the hospital. Baptist now maintains a list of employees who have four-wheel-drive vehicles that can be used to retrieve stranded employees.

- Take more pictures than you think you will need. If they had it to do over again, Baptist would have taken more pictures for its employee newsletter and other publications.

- Maintain a list of media and hospital staff telephone numbers at home as well as at the office. It will come in handy if you need to make calls from home in the middle of the night.

- In the event of a hurricane warning, plan to move computers that are in window offices out of harm's way well before the storm starts.

- Be prepared to receive busloads of residents from area nursing homes and assisted living facilities. Know how to reach key personnel at these facilities.

- If hospitals in your state do not have a statewide mutual aid system, consider organizing one. It should encompass nursing, allied health, engineering and food service. Baptist has launched such a system, with key contact information stored on a secure part of its website

CASE STUDY 4.4
STRIKE

At Highlands Regional Medical Center in rural southeastern Kentucky, District 1199 SEIU (Service Employees International Union—AFL-CIO) has represented the service, maintenance and technical employees for almost twenty years. Before 1999, the union had called one strike, in 1981. That strike was violent and lasted for 121 days.

Time passed, wounds healed and life went on. Subsequent contracts were negotiated every three years. Each time, there was talk of whether there would be a strike. But at the eleventh hour, a contract was always reached. In 1999, things were different.

That year, a new CEO had come on board. Administrative changes are one of the indications unions look for in determining strike targets. In January 1999, SEIU launched an effort to organize the nursing staff. The March vote result was challenged by the hospital. The collective bargaining process that began in April did not go well. The existing contract was set to expire on July 13. The deadline was extended, but to no avail. A strike involving service, maintenance and technical personnel was called for September 2.

Every department in the hospital was affected. Most patients in the 184-bed hospital were transferred to other facilities. Only one 12-bed unit and the emergency department were kept open. Managerial staff kept the facility running; they did everything from mop the floors to clean the bathrooms.

When the strike started, the contract proposal that was on the table had never been seen by the majority of Highland's employees. The union did not show it to the rank-and-file members. It was seen only by a few union leaders. More than 450 Highlands employees went out on strike without ever having read the contract proposal.

The hospital proposed health coverage at a cost of $7 per bimonthly pay period for individuals and $20 for families; the union demanded healthcare benefits at no cost to employees. The union also wanted more control over hospital management, including having a union representative present at every board meeting and union management of retirement funds. These demands were unacceptable to the hospital.

The hospital used several communications vehicles to convey the proposed contract terms to employees:

- Articles were printed in the local newspaper every week.
- Flyers were sent directly to employees' homes.
- Paid advertising included open letters to employees and to the community and included verbatim sections from the contract.

Continued on page 98

CASE STUDY 4.4

STRIKE *Continued from page 97*

- "Infomercials" were aired on local radio stations.
- A 10-minute video explaining contractual provisions was produced in-house and mailed to all employees.

During the strike, getting employees across the picket lines and into the hospital safely was a challenge. The hospital contracted with a security firm that brought in guards and vans. The guards stayed at a nearby hotel, which allowed hospital employees to use their parking lot. Employees were brought to work in vans driven by the guards. Van windows were darkened to prevent employees from being heckled by picketers. Guards were posted at each entrance to medical center property—armed only with video cameras. They filmed each vehicle that entered or exited the property. When picketers later alleged that cars had bumped or threatened them, the videos were used to prove those allegations false.

The strike was a real low point in the hospital's 30-year history. During negotiation sessions, reason and logic disappeared. State and federal mediators attempted to control the chaos, but sessions ended with little or no progress being made.

Inside the hospital, staff meals were relocated from the glass-enclosed Food Court to the basement hallway for added security. Meals—all free—were one of the high points of the employees' days. The emergency department never closed, even though ambulances and patients had to cross picket lines to get there. When a baby was saved after being brought into the ED near death from drowning, it was clear the effort to stay open had been worthwhile.

At first, the community reacted to the news of the strike with disbelief. Many voiced opinions as to who was at fault, but most people just wanted it to be over. As time passed and negotiations continued, management never deviated from their original message explaining the proposed contract terms.

When the 75-day strike finally ended, there were no winners. The hospital lost $4.5 million and both sides lost trust and respect. Damage from negative publicity in the community was incalculable. "It will never be the same as it was before," says Kathy Rubado, director of marketing and public relations for the hospital. "And it probably could have been prevented if employees had known what we were truly proposing."

LESSONS LEARNED

- Unions have resources—money *and* people—and they are not compelled to play by your guidelines. They have their own handbook; indeed, the union's campaign manual provides a step-by-step escalation strategy used to organize and lead employees to a strike.

- Union negotiations and strikes are public relations and communications wars. You will be in the trenches fighting for the life of your organization in one of the most difficult and costly situations you will ever face.

- Retain the best and most experienced legal counsel you can find. Specific labor negotiations experience is very important.

- In a strike situation, maintain an ongoing internal campaign to communicate your position on wages, health insurance premiums, contract labor, retirement benefits and other key issues. Consider using daily memos and e-mail messages, CEO focus group meetings, daily managers' meetings and direct mail to employees' homes.

- The first priority in a strike situation is to ensure the safety of all parties involved—especially patients and employees who cross the picket lines. Security may need to be increased. Hire a professional security company with experience in strike situations. If a strike is imminent, bring in security a minimum of two or three months in advance to protect physical plant and property. If your hospital plans to continue operations, you must ensure safe transportation for employees.

- Highlands Regional was concerned that its board of directors might become union targets at their homes or businesses, and union employees did, in fact, stage protests in the parking lots at some board members' businesses. Union representatives also showed up at a hospital board meeting, announcing that Highlands was their union hospital and demanding that the board give in to their wishes "or else."

- Educate managers about the terms being proposed in the contract. If managers understand the language in the contract and fully understand what is being proposed and why, they can be effective salespeople for getting your message across to employees. Employees usually go to their managers, not administration, to ask questions.

- If nurses are being targeted by the union for representation, they need to understand the benefits they currently have, what the hospital is proposing and what they stand to lose if they elect to have—or continue—union representation.

CASE STUDY 4.4

STRIKE *Continued from page 99*

- Keep your physicians informed through memos and special medical staff meetings. If you don't keep them informed, you can be sure that union information is being channeled directly to them from employees and union sympathizers in the community.

- It is critically important that your employees know what the organization is proposing in the contract and why. You must counter the flood of information—and misinformation— that employees will receive from the union.

- In dealing with the media:

    Be honest.

    Be aware that press releases probably will not be printed. Plan to disseminate your message by paid advertising.

    Be prepared for negative "letters to the editor" and respond appropriately. Also, be aware that some newspapers may refuse to print letters pertaining to the strike.

    Expect every interview with a hospital official to be followed by one with the most vocal union employee on the picket line. Know that reporters can also influence the way an interview is perceived by the comments they make when it is aired.

    Be aware that strikes can be a significant income opportunity for local media outlets. Highland Regional's media costs for strike-related newspaper and radio advertising were almost $100,000.

- In rural areas, do not count on local officials or law enforcement agencies to intervene on your behalf. Some police groups have union representation. Chances are that members of your local law enforcement agency live next door to your employees, not to your board members or your CEO.

- Know that *all* elected officials listen to voters—in other words, to your employees. As administrators and managers, you are greatly outnumbered. A fall election took place during the strike at Highlands Regional. Administrators watched out the windows as political candidates showed up on the picket lines to distribute campaign literature along with free pizza and soft drinks.

AFTER THE CRISIS IS OVER

5.1. OVERVIEW

On a practical level, when a crisis is over it is important to review, debrief and change your crisis communications plan in light of what you have learned. (*See Section 1.6.*) You will also want to consider the human dimension of the crisis—the effects it has on your colleagues and your community—and your role, as a communications professional, in mitigating those effects.

A crisis by its very nature is an incident that has a beginning, a middle and an end, at least from the hospital's perspective. But when is that ending? Is it when the last patient has been discharged? When the media coverage trails off and then stops? Often, the end of the crisis is not as clearcut as it may seem. Just as crises change the lives of individuals, they also leave their mark on organizational culture and community life. The changes wrought by crises are often complex and multifaceted.

In an internal crisis, the overriding need of the parties involved is for a fresh start, yet the energy to create it is usually in short supply. A threat to the organization's reputation may leave people hesitant to move forward—anxious to put the incident behind them but worried that the seeds of destruction are still there and still viable. A strike can leave all parties involved at once weary of present events and wary of the future. Successfully moving beyond an internal crisis demands more than a communications initiative; it can require authentic and far-reaching changes in organizational culture.

Living through a disaster—whether natural or manmade—is a different story. The hospital team that shares the experience can have a variety of reactions, ranging from avoiding any reminder of the crisis to retelling the story endlessly to developing post-traumatic stress disorder. Employees need recognition for the contributions that they have made, the selflessness they showed in staying at their posts despite worries about their own families and the unique, individual twists on a common theme that each person experienced. The people who share the crisis experience often develop new bonds or find their old bonds strengthened. But, for a few who harbor doubts about their own performance or regrets about what they did or did not do, the group accolades and camaraderie are a source of anxiety. And for those who have personally experienced loss as a result of the tragedy, the crisis goes on long after others have begun to let it go.

Community members often have intense and conflicting reactions as well. It is natural for the community to look to the hospital that provided shelter and medical help during the crisis for healing and solace afterwards. There may be groups that are in particular need of this support, such as relief workers and survivors and their families. Parents may also be looking for ways to explain the disaster to their children, help children cope with anxiety and depression and recognize when children need extra help.

For all of these reasons, the hospital's role—and that of the communicators—does not end when the disaster victims and the media go home.

5.2. RESPONDING TO A NATIONAL TRAGEDY: THE AFTERMATH OF SEPTEMBER 11, 2001

After the terrorist attacks of September 11 and the subsequent anthrax incidents, hospitals were called on to support their communities as perhaps never before. People all over the country experienced a sense of loss and grief, fear of an unknown enemy, and invisible threats to their health by anthrax, a previously little known disease. Sheryl Ray McLain, vice president, communications, at the Oklahoma Hospital Association, has given many presentations about the 1995 bombing of the Alfred P. Murrah Federal Building in Oklahoma City that killed 168 people. After September 11, McLain emphasized that healing is a long-term process. "Your communities are going to need you over the long haul for emotional support and healing. . . I don't think we'll have an idea for quite some time of the enormous emotional impact this will have on our nation. It is certainly an area in which hospitals and other health professionals can shine and demonstrate value to those in need."

New York- and Washington, DC-area hospitals in the crisis "epicenter" reached out to their communities in a variety of ways (Usner 2002).

- Nassau University Medical Center was quick to offer free walk-in trauma and grief counseling. Following is the text posted on the hospital's website on September 12 (www.ncmc.edu):

  > The entire local and national community has been emotionally shaken by the recent tragedies. The entire Department of Psychiatry at Nassau University Medical Center is available to anyone needing its services for trauma or grief counseling. The Departments of Pediatrics and Psychiatry and Psychology are also providing counseling for children and adolescents. There is no appointment needed—walk-ins are welcome from 8:00 a.m. to 6:00 p.m. today. Grief counseling will also be available at least for the rest of September. The sessions are free and confidential. For further information please call 572-6824.

- Long Island College Hospital paramedics spoke at local schools. One of the topics was *Do You Have to Be Dead to Be a Hero?* Management also participated in community town hall meetings and editorial meetings with local media outlets to educate them about bioterrorism.

- New York Methodist Hospital took a different tack to educate the community, by conducting "train the trainer" sessions on bioterrorism for community leaders. The hospital opted to reach out to people directly through its community organizations, so as not to create panic about anthrax and to reach a larger number of individuals.

- St. Vincent's Catholic Medical Centers staffed a mental health hotline 24 hours a day, seven days a week for three weeks. They also provided counseling to New York City Fire Department workers, children in lower Manhattan schools, and area corporations. And they stationed grief counselors to help travelers at New York's Kennedy Airport following the later airplane crash in Queens, NY. In the first 72 hours after September 11, they had approximately 6,000 visits to their family center, mostly for mental health counseling.

- Calvary Hospital, a hospice, conducted media interviews on coping with loss. Calvary expanded the use of its *Kids to Kids* video as a teaching tool in schools, addressing how children cope with bereavement.

- New York University Downtown Hospital was particularly hard hit, being so close to the World Trade Center. The neighborhood had no power or phone service for several days, and many staff had to stay at the hospital. In addition to feeding all hospital employees, the hospital staff made house calls and delivered meals to the homebound elderly in a housing development across from the hospital. They also provided meals and counseling for rescue workers, aided by a *New York Times* Foundation grant. To serve their large Chinese-speaking population and other non-English speakers, hospital staff gave multilingual community lectures that featured a historical perspective on bioterrorism. They provided counseling for employees of area businesses, both those directly and indirectly affected by the building collapse. The hospital also had to deal with unexpected attention, such as the 10,000 stuffed bears that arrived one day as a donation from an American Indian tribe from Oklahoma. And, recognizing the impact this would have on their hospital in the future, they made a documentary interviewing hospital staff on what they saw and experienced during the first crucial days.

- The District of Columbia Hospital Association sought to form a September 11 Response Coalition, and looked to a community partnership that was already in place through an End of Life Coalition, a partnership among area psychiatric hospitals, hospices, mental health groups and nonprofit clinics. The coalition provided crisis response training to healthcare professionals and those in helping professions, and served as a clearinghouse of community resources. It also established a general hotline and a teen hotline to aid area residents in need of support after the attacks. Its training focused on helping mental health professionals, teachers and clergy identify signs of post-traumatic stress disorder, and helping emergency room staff identify physical illnesses manifested from stress.

Because this tragedy was national in scope, hospitals and health systems throughout the country responded.

- St. Francis Hospital & Health Centers in Indianapolis activated their crisis response teams. A mental health counselor was assigned to area schools. Information about anthrax and mail safety was posted on the hospital website. Management participated in town forums with the post office, fire department, police department, utilities, schools and elected officials.

- Lake Forest Hospital, Lake Forest, IL, established a hotline staffed by registered nurses to answer questions about anthrax and related issues. The hospital also hosted a public forum on bioterrorism and community readiness and posted relevant information on its website.

As these examples demonstrate, it is important to partner with other organizations, including community agencies, schools and foundations, in your outreach efforts. Think about the relationships and connections you have in place that you could tap after a crisis. What resources exist? What funding is available?

5.3. THE LONG VIEW

Often, hospitals will sponsor events in the immediate crisis aftermath, such as blood drives, interfaith prayer services or memorial services. The events of September 11 and the following months expanded the roster of outreach activities in a variety of ways, as described in Section 5.2. But the healing process does not end when the time for such events is over.

There are several ways the hospital can reach out to the employees and the community to meet their needs in the long term.

- Help community members channel their grief in constructive ways by **educating the community** about safety practices that could prevent further tragedies. This may involve partnering with community agencies, schools and educational groups. When food poisoning sickened hundreds at an upstate New York county fair, Albany Medical Center took the lead in public education about prevention, symptoms of and treatment for food poisoning (*see Case Study 5.1*).

- Another constructive outlet for grief is through **advocacy** for laws and public policies that can reduce the risk of a similar tragedy recurring. After the Carrollton bus crash (*see Case Study 5.2*) in which 27 children and adults on a church bus were killed, Kosair Children's Hospital advocated for highway safety through encouraging seatbelt use, burn prevention and alcohol awareness. Hospital staff traveled with the young survivors to the state legislature where they testified in favor of stopping drunk driving and making highways safer.

- **Provide an appropriate setting** for community groups that seek to hold commemorative events. After the Carrollton Bus Crash, church and community groups organized such events around the anniversary date of the crash for years. Kosair Children's Hospital always made its facilities available and the staff who had taken care of the children always participated.

Finally, be open to the good that may come out of a crisis. When small, semirural Palm Drive Hospital in Sebastopol, CA, was slated for closure by corporate owner Columbia, the community rallied around the hospital and found a way to save the hospital from the wrecking ball. (*See Case Study 5.3.*)

As employees leave over a period of time, do not let the organizational memory of a crisis that has been pivotal in community life go with them. Create an archive that is dedicated to the original event and all that followed it. Appoint someone to maintain and preserve the archive. The anniversary of the incident is the natural time to plan commemorative events around it but it is not the only one. There is a health observance day dedicated to just about every imaginable health issue. The Society's *Health Observances and Recognition Days Calendar* provides a listing of days, weeks and months that focus on various health issues. Information is available on the Society website, www.stratsociety.org.

Regardless of the old, current and new ways crisis can strike a healthcare organization, not much will change in the way of *managing* crises. Preparedness, practice, alacrity, honesty and a willingness to constantly strive to improve will be the hallmarks of the organizations—and the communicators— most likely to succeed in any crisis. One thing we know for sure—crises will always be with us.

> *Thank Heaven! The crisis*
> *The danger, is past,*
> *And the lingering illness,*
> *The fever called "Living"*
> *Is conquered at last.*

Edgar Allan Poe (1809–1845)

CASE STUDY 5.1
FOOD POISONING AT THE COUNTY FAIR

Food poisoning can and does strike anywhere. And as Richard Puff, formerly associate director of public relations at Albany Medical Center (AMC), was to find out, often with devastating results. Just before the Labor Day weekend in 1999, it turned up in food consumed at the Washington County Fair in upstate New York.

As crises are wont to do, this one occurred just as most hospital administrators were preparing to leave for a long holiday weekend—at 3:30 p.m. on the Friday before Labor Day. Puff received a call from the hospital's infection control coordinator who reported that, over the previous two or three days, four children had been admitted to the hospital with classic symptoms of food poisoning—and had tested positive for *E. coli 0157: H7.*

An AMC physician had determined that all of the children had attended the county fair. She had already notified the appropriate state and local health officials. Puff was alerted by a staff member that the state health department would be issuing a media alert. This early warning turned out to be a key factor in AMC's ability to deal actively with the impending crisis.

At 6 p.m., the New York State Health Department released a news advisory to all regional media outlets advising people to seek medical attention immediately if they experienced any symptoms of food poisoning.

As the only tertiary care center in the region, AMC knew the media soon would be calling with requests to speak with experts on *E. coli*. A believer in offensive rather than defensive public relations, Puff took the initiative and offered the State Health Department an AMC expert to respond to media questions. The offer was accepted.

By 5:30 p.m., Richard Puff caught up with Martha Lepow, M.D., just as she was leaving for the weekend, and explained the situation. She said, "Whatever you need, I'll be there." When the first media call came in, Puff was ready. He invited the media to a news briefing at 6:30 p.m. (three hours after first learning of the problem). The information released was limited to the number of children being treated along with their ages and genders in addition to general information about *E. coli.*

Because the children were in serious or critical condition, Puff thought it would be inappropriate to intrude on the parents' privacy by asking them for permission to release names at that time. Later that night, Dr. Lepow went to a local television station studio for a live interview on the late news.

Meanwhile, communications systems were put into place. The emergency department set up a tracking and surveillance mechanism to ensure that epidemiology would be notified if patients arrived with the appropriate symptoms. Epidemiology faxed or called public relations three times each day with updated statistics: at 10 a.m. (in time for the news at noon), at 4 p.m. (for the evening news) and again at 9 p.m. (for the late news).

This schedule was given to the media, thereby forestalling any chance of having to contend with a constant, sporadic and perhaps disruptive stream of media inquiries and constantly changing answers.

At the time, the hospital had no way of knowing that the crisis would go on for the next four weeks and produce a total of 781 confirmed or suspected cases of E. coli, 71 hospitalizations (at several area hospitals) and two deaths.

One of the two deaths occurred in AMC's Pediatric Intensive Care Unit (PICU) the day after the crisis began. With this death, the case became a matter of public record. Later that evening, the girl's parents, who remained in the PICU at a younger daughter's bedside, saw the "teaser" on the TV set in the room: "Little girl dies of food poisoning. Details at 11."

Fortunately, the girls' father, rather than being upset by the sudden publicity, welcomed the chance to talk about his daughter. He didn't want her to be a faceless statistic; he didn't want her to be forgotten. So he called the TV station and volunteered to do an interview.

As Dr. Lepow drove home from the TV studio after doing a second interview on Saturday night, she called Puff at home to say that the reporter who had interviewed her had mentioned that the father who lost his daughter had contacted the station and offered to do an interview at 12:30 p.m. Puff called the father, offered his condolences and made sure the parents didn't feel compelled to do any media interviews. The father said he understood, but wanted to proceed anyway.

So, shortly after midnight, Puff accompanied the parents to a room adjacent to the hospital lobby where a local TV reporter conducted an on-camera interview. The reporter handled the interview well and refrained from sensationalizing the case. On the way back to the PICU, Puff explained that once the interview was aired, other media would ask to interview family members.

The father asked Puff for advice; Puff recommended holding a news conference. The interview aired Sunday, and as Puff had predicted, calls flooded in from other local media outlets, wire services and even New York City media.

Puff set up a news conference at AMC for Monday morning. After a brief introduction and an update on the latest numbers of admissions and patient conditions, Puff turned the meeting over to the girl's father, who spent 45 minutes recounting the hour-by-hour experience of losing his daughter.

Continued on page 108

CASE STUDY 5.1

FOOD POISONING AT THE COUNTY FAIR *Continued from page 107*

As sad as this story was, it was not the only drama unfolding in the hospital's PICU. There were a dozen children with food poisoning in the medical center, all in serious condition. Greg McGarry, director of public relations at the Medical Center, met with all the families at once to discuss media relations issues and to reassure them, in the wake of the earlier news conference, that the hospital would *not* give out any patient names without the *express written consent* of the parents.

Puff asked if any of the families wanted to talk with the media and explained that his staff was there to facilitate media interviews—or to shield the families from unwanted media attention. None of the families wanted any contact with the media and were relieved that the hospital was actively working to protect their privacy.

Part of the advice McGarry offered was a suggestion that the families ask their relatives, friends and neighbors to refrain from talking with reporters. (Later, after their children had recovered, many of these families did step forward and talked with the media, but at the height of their own personal crises, they did not want to do so.)

To deal with the hundreds of calls to the emergency department about food poisoning, public relations staff set up a telephone hotline with recorded information about the signs and symptoms of *E. coli*. This helped relieve the phone congestion.

When the national media (including CNN and the *New York Times*) entered the fray, simply providing daily statistical updates wasn't enough. Puff knew that a fresh approach was needed.

To start, he knew the media needed visuals. Videotape of children in the PICU from a fundraising campaign (with signed patient releases already on file) was released to the media. Puff made it clear that the unit shown in the film was the place where the young *E. coli* victims were being treated, but that the children in this tape were *not* the *E. coli* patients.

Next, Puff set out to broaden the scope of the coverage. He knew the media would welcome new story ideas. Why not do a story on the pediatric dialysis service? Fourteen of the 71 *E. coli* patients had developed hemolytic uremic syndrome, a serious complication of *E. coli* that causes acute kidney failure. All were receiving dialysis services at AMC, the sole provider in the area, so the story was topical and relevant.

The microbiology laboratory represented another positive story opportunity—this time about the crucial role the laboratory staff played in treating patients affected by food poisoning. The same strategy was used for a subsequent story about the PICU. Even when "hard news" stories became less frequent, interest remained high. The Medical Center created opportunities to shine the spotlight on its staff, to thank them and honor them.

As part of its communications strategy, AMC did more than respond to the crisis—it capitalized on an opportunity to communicate about the regional tertiary care role of the Medical Center and the advanced capabilities of its staff.

AMC also played an important public education role, talking about prevention, symptoms and treatment for food poisoning.

LESSONS LEARNED

- You can fulfill your first duty to safeguard the privacy of the patient and the patient's family while *simultaneously* meeting the media's need for information. If you are forthcoming about providing the information you *do* have—which you *can* release—the media will respect your boundaries.

- Be proactive. Don't wait for the media to find you. Anticipate their needs and questions and go to them.

- Press conferences need not be frenetic and adversarial affairs. Facilitate opportunities for people to tell their own stories in genuine and meaningful ways.

- Have a podium sign showing the hospital's name and logo so the name is clearly visible during news conferences for purposes of still photographs and TV news coverage.

- If you find yourself dealing with a long-term crisis, look for ways to generate positive publicity through coverage that spotlights the strengths of your staff and your organization. This also helps the media meet their goals for generating news stories, thereby creating a "win-win" situation that will further enhance your media relations.

- In an ongoing crisis, establish a routine for your communications (as much as possible) to minimize disruption and misinformation. Let the media know that updates will be issued at certain times and then stick to that schedule.

- Long before a crisis occurs, establish relationships with physicians, nurses and other clinical and support staff throughout the organization. The mutual trust and the communications channels you have developed will make all the difference in times of crisis.

CASE STUDY 5.1

CASE STUDY 5.2
THE CARROLLTON BUS CRASH

Imagine being awakened at 1 a.m. on a Sunday by a call from a reporter who informs you that at least 15 children have just died in a church bus crash. This was exactly the situation Charlotte Tharp, then the director of public relations at Alliant Health System, owner of Kosair Children's Hospital in Louisville, KY, had to deal with on May 16, 1988. The crisis eventually involved the deaths of 27 people—most of them children.

What came to be known as the Carrollton Bus Crash started when a drunk driver in a pickup truck, going the wrong direction on a highway, struck a church activity bus returning from a trip to an amusement park in Cincinnati. The collision sparked a deadly explosion.

Within minutes of Tharp's arrival at the hospital, the first two patients arrived. (Eventually, 11 would be admitted.)

Soon after, parents started calling to find out if their child was among the survivors. The hospital shared patients' names and other information with the police and other hospitals where victims had been taken. However, names were not given to the news media until families gave permission.

The priority was to do whatever it took to make sure all family members knew what had happened to their loved ones as soon as possible.

Even while assembling a roster of accident victims (created by contacting other area hospitals), Tharp conducted brief interviews with the media. Although she was able to handle all the media relations herself, she stayed at the hospital a full 24 hours to accommodate reporters who wanted to talk with someone who had been at the hospital when the first accident victims arrived.

Media interest in the story stretched on for days and weeks. Local reporters and Cincinnati-based reporters developed a rapport with many of the families as children returned for rehab and follow-up visits.

Although Tharp could not have known it at the time, the commemorative events surrounding this tragic accident would continue for years. The Carrollton bus crash was a defining event in the life of the community. Virtually all the commemorative events were organized by church and community groups, not by the hospital itself. But, Kosair Children's was the natural focal point to which everyone returned. The hospital always made its facilities available and the staff who had taken care of the Carrollton kids always participated.

Kosair Children's found other meaningful ways to honor those who died in the crash. The hospital continued its leadership in advocating for highway safety through seatbelt use, burn prevention and alcohol awareness. Hospital staff even traveled with the young survivors to the state legislature where they testified in favor of stopping drunk driving and making highways safer.

The hospital also conducts a program for area teachers focused on helping children return to school after a traumatic injury, helping kids who are "different" and helping other children accept those who were scarred and disfigured.

LESSONS LEARNED

- Do not try to handle a crisis alone. Even though you may be able to handle the demands of a marathon 24-hour shift, keep in mind that the demands of the crisis might continue for days—or even weeks.

- To satisfy media needs for first-person observation, try to have more than one person willing and able to share their experience with reporters in the early hours and days of the crisis, when caregivers may be too tired or too busy.

- Be flexible in sharing information with other hospitals, law enforcement authorities and groups directly involved. Patient privacy protections are not intended to impede efforts to determine the location and medical condition of accident or disaster victims.

- Understand the long-term emotional and psychological dynamics of a crisis. It does not end when the last patient is discharged. Those who survived the crisis—and those who cared for them—will form a new community within the larger hospital community.

- After the acute phase of a crisis is over, look for a "silver lining." There may be opportunities for your organization to initiate prevention or public health efforts and work with concerned individuals, families and community groups.

CASE STUDY 5.2

CASE STUDY 5.3
RURAL HOSPITAL AVERTS CLOSURE

For years, 49-bed Palm Drive Hospital served as the only local access to 24-hour emergency, acute care and other medical services for residents of Sebastopol, CA.

The emergency room at Palm Drive served 10,000 people a year, including many who probably would not have survived the trip on secondary roads to the nearest larger hospital. In fact, in times of flooding it is difficult to travel from parts of rural western Sonoma County to the larger hospitals in Santa Rosa.

Furthermore, Palm Drive Hospital is the only hospital in the western part of the county that has the resources to provide emergency healthcare in times of crisis. Compounding the problem, without the presence of the hospital, physicians who maintained practices in the community probably would move their offices elsewhere.

When the hospital's owner—Columbia HCA—said it would close the hospital in two months, residents of Sebastopol decided to fight back. In November 1998, they held an emergency town hall meeting, attended by nearly 500 people. Nine people, including members of the Chamber of Commerce, Rotary Club and local businesspeople, quickly formed the West County HealthCare Foundation. Palm Drive had neither public relations nor development staff, so all the work ahead would fall to volunteers.

The fledgling Foundation knew its success depended on generating community interest and understanding about the urgency of the situation. In doing so, the community used every tool at its disposal from bake sales to bond issues. On December 11, the Foundation staged a candlelight vigil that drew nearly 200 people and generated $2,500 in "seed" money. Within several days a limited liability company—"35 for Palm Drive"—was formed and quickly raised $1 million in pledges from local businesses and citizens. (In all, $3 million was raised.)

Other community members were scrambling behind the scenes to obtain tax-exempt status for the Foundation so donors could receive full tax benefits for their donations.

A grassroots fundraising effort was under way at the same time. Car washes, bake sales, polenta dinners, "crab feeds" and benefit dances filled an already busy holiday season calendar.

Everyone participated. In one "dream" public relations moment, a young boy came to a community meeting with $100 in small bills clutched in an envelope. His mother said her son had visited Palm Drive's emergency room so many times, he felt he had to donate his lawn-mowing earnings to save the hospital.

Shortly after the New Year, the Foundation asked for—and received—an extension on the closing date from Columbia HCA. Through February, fundraising events continued almost every weekend.

In the meantime, community members and Columbia HCA agreed on a sale price and on February 28, 1999, the sale closed. The next day, Palm Drive started its new life as a community not-for-profit hospital.

But the story did not end there. The very same managed care pressures that had compelled Columbia to close the hospital still plagued Palm Drive. The hospital limped along on a breakeven basis for the rest of the year. Volunteer board members realized they needed to develop strategies to turn things around. None of the four physicians and five local businesspeople had any experience actually *operating* a hospital. They knew they needed help. First, they promoted a talented nurse-manager to serve as chief administrative officer. In an innovative move, they sought additional management support from a top executive of a Santa Rosa hospital, who kept his job in Santa Rosa and came to Sebastopol on a part-time basis.

Then, in December 1999 just when things were looking up, disaster struck again: the hospital's leading surgeon retired and along with him went significant income he would have generated for the hospital. The losses were so great that Palm Drive once again was faced with closing its doors by midyear. To survive, the hospital borrowed money from local banks to meet payroll and stay afloat. The hospital then hired a turnaround specialist and CEO and crafted a survival strategy centering on physician recruitment. At the same time, the concept of creating a Health Care District supported with property taxes was explored. It could be done, but under California state law it required no less than the approval of two-thirds of the voters in a special election.

Together, the Foundation and the limited liability company made plans to gather enough support to form the district and issue $5.9 million in general obligation bonds. It was a daunting task; no new healthcare district had been approved in California for 25 years. It was a long shot, at best, but to community members, it was worth it.

For the second time in a year, a massive communications effort was launched—this time the focus was on getting out the vote. And once again, the effort was rewarded—the referendum sailed through with a 91 percent majority. The newly formed healthcare district duly purchased the hospital and repaid $500,000 in loans to the local bank.

CASE STUDY 5.3

Continued on page 114

CASE STUDY 5.3
RURAL HOSPITAL AVERTS CLOSURE *Continued from page 113*

LESSONS LEARNED

- Some employee attrition is inevitable. It was a difficult year for Palm Drive employees. Some took advantage of the severance packages offered by Columbia HCA and left. But many of those who stayed threw themselves into the rescue effort in a variety of ways.

- Make sure that all employees are kept up-to-date on the latest developments. Palm Drive held monthly employee forums on all shifts.

- Find other ways to communicate with employees as well. Palm Drive sent regular e-mail updates to all employees and created payroll stuffers with messages from the CEO. Provide opportunities for employees to come together informally around happy occasions, such as monthly potluck birthday celebrations.

- Take advantage of unrelated publicity opportunities that give you a chance to communicate your primary messages through the media. In Palm Drive's case, a nursing shortage provided opportunities for the media to convey their main messages:

  - We are still here.

  - We are still operating at full capacity.

- Never underestimate the power of a community that values its hospital—citizens are a tremendous asset in times of crisis.

- A hospital threatened with closure may benefit from a combination of strategies, including grassroots fundraising, venture capital financing and even conversion to public ownership.

- Do not forget to support the employees. Keep them informed every step of the way. Use face-to-face communication whenever possible.

■ When a closure has been averted, it does not mean the crisis is over. The market pressures that brought about the closure threat are likely still there. Be prepared to move into a different phase of the crisis.

■ Expect numerous ups and downs over the course of several months or even years. Pay attention to stress management.

A postscript:

All of the communications efforts in this case study were coordinated by Judy Farrell, a local real estate agent—and concerned citizen—who took an unofficial three-month leave of absence during the height of the crisis to devote all her time and energy to rescuing Palm Drive. When the dust settled, Farrell returned to her real estate practice, but it just wasn't the same—*she* wasn't the same—and today, Farrell serves as Palm Drive's first official director of development—and a successful one at that. Only a few months into her tenure, Farrell was instrumental in securing a $400,000 grant for community outreach, an effort initiated by a volunteer Fund Development Committee in mid-1999.

SOURCES

Advanced Public Speaking Institute. 2002. "Public Speaking: Tips for Television, Videotape, and Videoconferencing." [Online article]. Jan. www.public-speaking.org.

Alcorn, S. 2001. "Internal Crisis Communications in a New World." *Spectrum* Nov./Dec., 8-9.

American Hospital Association. 2001. "Nearly three-fifths of hospitals have Web sites, AHA survey finds." [Online news brief]. *AHA News Now*. Oct. 29. www.ahanews.com.

Davis & Company. 2000. "Traits of Great Communicators." [Online article]. www.davisandco.com.

Geisinger Health System. 2000. "Media Communications Procedures." [Internal communication].

Herman, M. and B. Oliver. 2002. "A primer for crisis management." *Risk Management* 49(1): 48.

Joint Commission on Accreditation of Healthcare Organizations. 1998. *Sentinel Event Alert*, Issue 4, May 11. [Online article]. www.jcaho.org.

_____. 2001."Mobilizing America's Healthcare Reservoir. Special Issue: Emergency Management in the New Millennium." [Online article]. *Joint Commission Perspectives* 21 (12). www.jcrinc.com.

_____. 2002. *Sentinel Events Statistics*. [Online data]. Jan. 23. www.jcaho.org.

Medical College of Ohio. 2001. *Media Training Guide*. Toledo, OH: Medical College of Ohio.

_____. 2001. *Reporter's Notebook*. Toledo, OH: Medical College of Ohio.

Medsafe, Inc. 2001. "Aftermath: lessons learned about emergency preparedness from the September 11 crisis." [Online article]. Oct. www.medsafe.com.

Regan, S. 2001. "Using Technology to Enhance Crisis Communications." *Spectrum* Nov./Dec., 6-7.

Society for Healthcare Strategy and Market Development. 2001. *Guidelines for Releasing Information on the Condition of Patients*. Chicago: American Hospital Association.

St. Francis Hospital & Health Centers. 2001. "Disaster/Crisis Categories." [Online information]. www.stfrancishospitals.org.

_____. 2001. "Disaster/Crisis Guidelines." [Online information]. www.stfrancishospitals.org.

Usner, P. 2002. "Communicating with Communities in Crisis: What You Can Do as a Leader in Your Community AFTER the Immediate Crisis Passes." Presentation to the American College of Healthcare Executives. Jan.

DO'S AND DON'TS OF EMERGENCY PUBLIC RELATIONS

During an emergency, DO

- Attend to the emergency.
- Release only verified information.
- Promptly alert press of relief and recovery operations.
- Escort the press everywhere on the emergency site.
- Have a designated spokesperson.
- Keep accurate records and logs of all inquiries and news coverage.
- Try to find out and meet media deadlines.
- Provide equal opportunities and facilities for print and electronic media.
- Have a clear idea of what can and cannot be released.
- Carefully coordinate planning and implementation of public relations activities with other aspects of the crisis plan.
- Spotlight heroes.
- Identify and monitor "troublemakers."
- Deal with rumors swiftly.
- Centralize all information.
- Consider recording questions, comments, etc.—have a scribe.

During an emergency, DON'T

- Release information that would violate the confidentiality of patients.
- Release any information unless it has been cleared by the communications department or the primary crisis team.
- Idly speculate on the causes of the emergency.
- Speculate on the resumption of normal operations.
- Speculate on the outside effects of the emergency.
- Interfere with the legitimate duties of the media.
- Permit unauthorized spokespersons to comment to the media.
- Attempt to cover up, or purposely mislead the media.
- Place blame for the emergency.

Guidelines for Releasing Information on the Condition of Patients

Introduction

Hospitals and health systems are responsible for protecting the privacy and confidentiality of their patients and patient information. The Health Insurance Portability and Accountability Act of 1996 (HIPAA) mandated regulations that govern privacy standards for healthcare information. HIPAA regulations specify the purposes for which information may and may not be released without authorization from the patient. This document updates the 1997 edition of the *Guide for the Release of Information on the Condition of Patients* to be consistent with HIPAA regulations. In addition, this document provides overall policy guidance about release of patient information.

This information is provided only as a guideline. Consult with legal counsel before finalizing any policy on the release of patient information. Also, be aware that healthcare facilities must comply with state privacy laws. Contact your legal counsel or your state hospital association for further information about the application of state and federal medical privacy laws on the release of patient information.

Condition and Location of Patients: What You May Release and to Whom

- **Inquiries must contain the patient's name—unless the inquiry comes from clergy.** Information about the condition and location of an inpatient, outpatient or emergency department patient may be released *only if the inquiry specifically contains the patient's name*. No information is to be given if a request does not include a specific patient's name. This includes inquiries from the press.

  Inquiries from the clergy are an exception. HIPAA privacy regulations expressly permit hospitals to release the patient's name, location in the hospital, general condition and religion to clergy members, so long as the patient has not told you *not* to release the information. Clergy do not need to ask for the individual by name. It is important to note that hospitals are not required to ask about patients' religious affiliations and patients are not required to supply that information.

- As long as the patient has not requested that information be withheld, **you may release the patient's one-word condition and location without obtaining prior patient authorization.**

⅃ *Condition*. For the one-word condition, use the terms "undetermined," "good," "fair," "serious" or "critical." See the *Definitions of Patient Conditions* section of this document for an explanation of terms.

The death of a patient may be reported to the authorities by the hospital, as required by law. Typically, a report will be made after efforts have been made to notify the next-of-kin. Information about the cause of death must come from the patient's physician, and its release must be approved by a legal representative of the deceased. This means that hospitals cannot share information with the media on the specifics about sudden, violent or accidental deaths, as well as deaths from natural causes, without the permission of the decedent's next-of-kin or other legal representative.

⅃ *Location*. The patient's location may be included in the hospital directory to facilitate visits by friends and family as well as delivery of flowers and gifts. However, as a matter of policy, the patient's location should *not* routinely be given to the media.

Although HIPAA does not expressly prohibit disclosure of patients' room location to the media (because the media are accorded the same access to information as other callers), this omission was not intended as a loophole to give journalists access to celebrity or other patients who do not wish them to have it. To safeguard patient privacy, it is recommended that hospitals adopt or maintain policies prohibiting disclosure of patient location to the media without patient permission. Furthermore, the media should not contact patients directly. Instead they should request an interview through a public relations or other designated hospital representative. Hospitals may deny the media access to the patient if it is determined that the presence of photographers or reporters would aggravate the patient's condition or interfere with patient care.

A representative should accompany the media at all times while they are in the hospital. Hospitals may deny the media access to any area at their discretion, including (but not limited to) operating rooms, intensive care units, maternity units, emergency departments, psychiatric departments, nurseries, pediatric units and substance abuse units.

BEYOND THE ONE-WORD CONDITION: MEDIA ACCESS TO PATIENTS

The following activities require written authorization from the patient:

Drafting a detailed statement (i.e., anything beyond the one-word condition) for approval by the patient or the patient's legal representative
Taking photographs of patients
Interviewing patients

In general, if the patient is a minor, permission for any of these activities must be obtained from a parent or legal guardian. Under certain circumstances, minors can authorize disclosure of information without parental approval or notification. State laws may vary.

Condition and Location of Patients: When You Should *Not* Release Any Information

- **Patients can "opt out" of providing information altogether.**
  The hospital has a responsibility to tell patients what information will be included in the hospital directory and to whom that information will be disclosed. The patient has the option to expressly state that he or she does not want information released—including confirmation of his or her presence in the facility.

- **Don't release information that could embarrass or endanger patients.**
  Spokespersons should not report any information that may embarrass a patient. Situations where room location information could embarrass patients include (but are not limited to) admission to a psychiatric or substance abuse unit; admission to an obstetrics unit following a miscarriage, ectopic pregnancy or other adverse outcome; or admission to an isolation room for treatment of an infectious disease. In addition, when knowledge of a patient's location could potentially endanger that individual (i.e., the hospital has knowledge of a stalker or abusive partner), no information of any kind should be given, including confirmation of the patient's presence at the facility.

- **Consider other applicable federal laws.**
  Be aware that federal laws prohibit hospitals from releasing any information regarding a patient being treated for alcohol or substance abuse. These include the Comprehensive Alcohol Abuse and Alcoholism Prevention, Treatment and Rehabilitation Act of 1970; the Drug Abuse Office and Treatment Act of 1972; and 42 CFR Part 2, 188. Other state laws may also apply.

- **Exercise good judgment in situations where patients can't express a preference.**
  In some cases, patients will not have had the opportunity to state a preference about having their information released. For example, a patient's medical condition may prevent hospital staff from asking about information preferences upon admission. In those circumstances, condition and location information should only be released if, *in the hospital's professional judgment*, releasing such information would be in the patient's best interest. Then, when the patient recovers sufficiently, the hospital must ask about information preferences. Each hospital should develop policies and procedures to guide staff in making these judgments.

Matters of Public Record

- **What is a matter of public record?**
  Matters of public record refer to situations that are reportable by law to public authorities, such as law enforcement agencies, the coroner or public health officer. While laws and/or regulations require healthcare facilities to report a variety of information to public authorities, it is not the responsibility of facilities to provide that information in response to calls or other inquiries

from the media or other parties, *including law enforcement officials*. Instead, such calls should be directed to the appropriate public authority.

Are public record cases different from other cases?
No. Patients who are involved in matters of public record have the same privacy rights as all other patients, as far as the hospital is concerned. The mode of transportation by which a patient arrives at the hospital should have no bearing on the hospital's approach to releasing information about the patient. The fact that someone has been transported to the hospital by a police or fire department from an accident, crime scene or fire is a matter of public record likely to be reported by those agencies. These public records may prompt media calls to the hospital requesting a patient's condition. Only the one-word condition should be given. For many hospitals, this may represent a change from previous policies.

There are numerous state statutes addressing reporting of incidents ranging from child abuse to gunshot wounds. The fact that a hospital has an obligation to report certain confidential information to a governmental agency does not make that information public and available to news reporters.

Refer media questions to the public entity (such as the coroner's office, police, fire or health department) that receives such reports. The public entity will be guided by the applicable statute as to whether it can release any or all of the information received.

Are celebrity cases different?
No. Celebrities, public figures and public officials are not subject to different standards than other patients when it comes to hospital policies for releasing information to the media.

RELEASING PATIENT INFORMATION IN DISASTER SITUATIONS

When feasible, notify the next-of-kin first.
While it is desirable to notify next-of-kin before releasing patient information, in disaster situations involving multiple casualties, it may be necessary to share patient information with other hospitals and/or rescue/relief organizations before the next-of-kin has been notified.

Don't hesitate to cooperate with other hospitals or relief agencies.
You may release patient information to other hospitals, healthcare facilities and relief agencies in situations where multiple facilities are receiving patients from one disaster. public relations representatives from different facilities are encouraged to cooperate and facilitate the exchange of information regarding patients' location and status. Specifically, you may disclose patient information to a public or private organization assisting in relief efforts for the purpose of notifying family members or others responsible for a patient's care about the patient's location, general condition or death.

- **When appropriate, release general information to help dispel public anxiety.**
  In highly charged situations such as disasters, the public may benefit from the release of general information when specific information is not yet releasable. For example, you might say that "the facility is treating four individuals as a result of the explosion." You may state the number of patients who have been brought to the facility by gender or by age group (adults, children, teenagers, etc.). This type of general information can help reduce undue anxiety.

- **Work effectively with the media.**
  Current information should be made available to the media as soon as possible. If information is not yet available or if next-of-kin has not been notified, all media inquiries should be logged and callbacks made as soon as information is releasable. A location should be provided for all media to gather so that information can be released in a news conference format that does not compromise patient privacy or the healthcare facility's need for added security in a disaster situation.

IX **Definitions of Patient Conditions**

> **Undetermined.** Patient awaiting physician and assessment.
>
> **Good.** Vital signs are stable and within normal limits. Patient is conscious and comfortable. Indicators are excellent.
>
> **Fair.** Vital signs are stable and within normal limits. Patient is conscious, but may be uncomfortable. Indicators are favorable.
>
> **Serious.** Vital signs may be unstable and not within normal limits. Patient is acutely ill. Indicators are questionable.
>
> **Critical.** Vital signs are unstable and not within normal limits. Patient may be unconscious. Indicators are unfavorable.

Clinicians find the "critical but stable" term useful when discussing cases among themselves, because it helps them differentiate patients who are expected to recover from those whose prognosis is worse. But a critical condition means that at least some vital signs are unstable, so this is inherently contradictory. The term "stable" *should not* be used as a condition. Furthermore, this term *should not* be used in combination with other conditions, which, by definition, often indicate a patient is unstable.

This information is available for purchase in convenient booklet format.
Call 800-AHA-2626 and ask for catalog no. 166851, or order online at www.ahaonlinestore.org.